Praise for *In Th*

"As one of the surgeons who provided care to Charlene, I can without reservation confirm that Charlene's journey has been a truly remarkable and miraculous path of recovery. Here she details every grueling physical, psychological, and emotional step she has taken as she has responded to the challenge of re-defining her life. This is a must read for anyone who values the human capacity for recovery and growth!"
—Michael Peck, MD, FACS, former president of the Board of Trustees of the American Burn Association

"In this moving, vulnerable memoir, Pell offers an enduring contribution to the testimony of human resilience . . . Pell's bold, inspiring memoir challenges readers to deeper empathy and to confront preconceived notions and biases."
—BookLife Reviews

"Charlene Pell has given us an inspiring, uplifting, motivating book about overcoming unthinkable loss and adversity. After getting burned, disfigured, and disabled by a catastrophic accident that essentially melted her lovely face and hands, she shows gob-smacking grit, fortitude, focus, character, confidence, and faith.

"And she needs every bit of it, because alongside her daunting physical and emotional recovery—all the pain, surgeries, and rehab, and the undoing of so much of her identity—this former 'looker' must now also cope with the reactions of people who either stare at her or can't stand to look at her, let alone deal with her.

"But this riveting page-turner does something else as well, something perhaps even more unique: when Pell describes managing her day-to-day, we get to observe and decode her brilliance, both as a big-picture strategist with long-term goals and a scrappy, skillful, wily tactician, maneuvering from step to step to stay on track, get back on track when derailed, and keep unlikely people on her side. This is a master class in strategy.

"*In This Altered Body* is a book for anyone with a big challenge, not just burn survivors and the people who love them, although they surely will go nuts for it. But no one will want to put this book down. It's a great read, with powerful lessons in how to get where you need to be, all the while honoring your beautiful inner self."

—Belleruth Naparstek, psychotherapist, author, and founder
of Health Journeys, a guided imagery audio library

"This engrossing memoir of surviving a horrific plane crash and a series of crushing life changes shows how persistence and a willingness to try can make all the difference. Charlene Pell never gave up. She's a forceful role model for transforming tragedy into an inspiration for others."

—Katherine Ramsland, bestselling author
of *Confession of a Serial Killer*

"It is not often that I open a memoir and can't put it down. This stunning book provides an opening into the lives and souls of people who, because of severe burn injury, often live on the periphery of our society. Charlene does this by skillfully sharing her own journey of healing from severe burns—healing both physically and psychologically. Her perceptive insight and engaging style capture her experience in a way that is courageous, compassionate, and compelling. Charlene's narrative of survival is not only a testament to her own resilience but also a lesson to all of us as we connect with the vagaries of life."

—Dave Sluyter, former CEO of the Fetzer Institute

"I was in awe of Charlene from the very first moment she introduced herself to us at the ABA meeting in 1996. My awe for her has increased substantially since reading her memoir. My husband, son, and I have all been hospitalized for burn injuries, and Charlene's detailed and articulate descriptions resonated profoundly with me as she unraveled her incredible experience of the plane crash, her tips and strategies for her recovery, and how she subsequently found love again, which changed her life. Not only will this amazing and remarkable woman's experience leave you in awe as it did me (yet again!), but her story will give untold hope, inspiration, and encouragement to those who are disfigured or suffering any type of physical 'difference.'"

—Delwyn Breslau, burn survivor advocate, founder of the Burn Support Group, and the wife of Alan Breslau, the late founder of the Phoenix Society

"A beautiful book from an utterly beautiful human. Charlene illustrates how to turn tragedy into triumph, through a life of devotion to others. Whether you have a facial difference or not, this book will help you to do the same."

—Phyllida Swift, CEO of Face Equality International

"Charlene's memoir provides a timely, universal, and hopeful message for our society. She addresses the importance of remaining human and honoring the personhood of each individual regardless of the circumstance. By sharing the horror and reality of her circumstances, she helps us understand the essence of being and remaining human. I am the nurse who asked, 'Can we create a place of healing that helps her transcend beyond her physical limitations?' and Charlene eloquently answered the question with a resounding *yes*.

"By courageously sharing her vulnerabilities, she has gifted us with the complex path that must be understood for her or any person to find the resilience to transcend. The complexity of the path is grounded in the ability for us to remain human and to express and pass forward love, kindness, and compassion, which are evident within her personhood and those walking with her on this journey.

"Each page of this book is filled with subtle and obvious pearls of wisdom from her story. As a nurse, I learned more about my accountability and enjoyed learning about Charlene's."

—Bonnie Wesorick, RN, MSN, FAAN, DPNAP, author
of *Polarity Thinking in Healthcare*, and eponym for
The Bonnie Wesorick Center for Healthcare Transformation
at Grand Valley State University in Michigan

"This book is a deep dive into Charlene's healing journey and what happened not just to her after the injury, but also to those around her: her family, friends, and even hospital staff. Charlene is a shining example of someone who never gave up hope, and who continues to strive to have a full and meaningful life. Her book is full of wisdom for every stage of burn recovery and a must-read for anyone affected by a burn injury, as well as for anyone who wants to understand what it takes to 'find yourself' after trauma."

—Barbara-Anne Hodge, chair of the Mamingwey
Burn Society and board member of the
Canadian Burn Survivors Community

In This
Altered Body

In This Altered Body

A Survivor's Story of
Resilience and Love

CHARLENE PELL

FACING
FORWARD
BOOKS

Published by Facing Forward Books, Greensboro, North Carolina
facingforwardinc.org
charlenepell.com

Edited and designed by Girl Friday Productions
www.girlfridayproductions.com

Cover design: Emily Weigel
Project management: Kristin Duran
Editorial production: Janice Lee and Jaye Whitney Debber
Image credits: cover © Joey Seawell Photography; p. 91 © Dr. Michael Kelly; p. 173 © Podhurst Orseck, PA; p. 192 © Extercamp Photography; p. 194 © Joey Seawell Photography

ISBN (hardcover): 979-8-9900340-2-0
ISBN (paperback): 979-8-9900340-0-6
ISBN (ebook): 979-8-9900340-1-3

Library of Congress Control Number: 2024904391

First edition

In loving memory of my mom, "DP," and to my sister, Melissa; their unwavering love, support, and encouragement sustained me through this life-altering ordeal. And to my beloved husband, CH, who sees and loves me just as I am and makes everything possible and worthwhile.

Contents

CHAPTER ONE

Another "Normal" Day

The dying must often feel this way—steaming along just fine, while on ahead someone has torn up the rails.

Annie Dillard

Fort Lauderdale, Florida, March 25, 1994

Rays of sunlight streamed through the transom window of the ladies' restroom at the Fort Lauderdale Executive Airport, causing my diamond tennis bracelet to glimmer—and sparking, once again, my unease. Just that morning, while dressing for work, I'd paused when reaching into my jewelry box for this bracelet. Clasping it around my wrist usually made me feel wrapped in my fiancé's love. Roger had given it to me at my surprise fortieth birthday party.

That morning, though, an unsolicited thought had attacked me.

I shouldn't wear this bracelet today. If something happens, I want my bracelet to go to Melissa.

Why would I even think of this? Of course, the bracelet would go to Melissa. My only sister meant the world to me. In 1986, a horrible automobile crash had left her as a ghost of the stunning, fit, fun-loving woman she had been. We'd always been close, but we became even closer after she moved in with me so I could help her. Whatever I had, I wanted to share with her—in life and in death.

But that day, I'd been gripped by an omen of my own death, not hers, and such dark thoughts were uncharacteristic for me. Shaking them off, I finished changing into the short shorts, tank top, and tennis shoes that would keep me cool and comfortable during the flight to Cat Island. Back at my car, I placed my work clothes in the trunk, took off the bracelet, and tucked it into the pocket of my red double-breasted top.

I headed to the tarmac, where I found Roger performing a preflight inspection of his private, nine-passenger, twin-engine airplane. He once told me that in the four decades he'd been flying, he'd never failed to do this inspection. Of course, flying in a small private plane carried risk on any day, but this particular aircraft had been the source of several troubling occurrences during our recent flights to Cat Island. Four times over the past two years, as we approached the small airport in Rock Sound to clear Bahamian customs, the position indicator light for the right landing gear, meant to warn us if the landing gear wasn't in the down-and-locked position, had failed to illuminate on the instrument panel.

It was unnerving. It required Roger to perform a "go-around," wherein he would abandon the approach to land and circle the small airport, doing a flyby of the air traffic control tower so that the controllers could see whether the landing gear was extended. As we circled the airport, Roger would radio the air traffic controllers and ask them to confirm that the landing gear was down. But even if a controller could tell him that the landing gear was down, the controller could not verify that it was successfully locked into its extended position, so there remained the possibility that the gear could collapse from the weight of the airplane during the landing. So far, we'd been lucky and landed safely—even on runways without a control tower to reassure us. The maintenance company for the plane had insisted that the problem was a malfunction with the indicator switch, not the landing gear itself. Still, it was enough to cause me to feel uneasy about flying. But Roger reassured me. "In the unlikely event that the hydraulics fail to lower the gear," he said, "I can crank the gear down by hand."

It was getting late, and we had to land on Cat Island before dusk as there were no lights on the runway.

"Charlena, ready to go to the island?" Roger asked, standing up from examining the tires. Sporting a panama hat, shorts, polo shirt, sunglasses, and white boat shoes, he was as robust and rugged as a sailor, his face and arms sunburned, his short white hair thinning on top. An irresistible dimple sat squarely in the center of his chin. This adventurous, confident man could sail a yacht, fly an airplane, prepare a gourmet meal, and do just about anything. For over twenty years, he'd owned and operated the most successful wholesale truck dealership in South Florida. He worked long hours but never seemed to show it.

On the other hand, I was ready for a break and a margarita. The stress of an exceptionally demanding month as vice president of communications for the Design Center of the Americas had zapped my energy—what with conferences, advertising deadlines, and the dismissal of a newly hired, disappointing employee. I smiled and said, "Relaxation is exactly what I'm ready for."

I climbed the steps that folded out from the only door, located in the fuselage behind the wing and fuel tanks, and entered the cabin. I grabbed a few trade magazines from my satchel and settled into the copilot's seat. Roger climbed aboard, raised the steps, and secured the door for takeoff. We fastened our seat belts and began taxiing down the runway. As always, Roger spoke into the headset: "N7929 Quebec, requesting clearance to take off."

"Roger," the air traffic controller said. "N7929Q, you are cleared for takeoff on runway eight niner." Pilots and air traffic controllers say "niner" to avoid any misunderstanding of the number. "Nine" and "five" can sound alike on radio transmissions.

Roger manipulated various instruments and put the airplane in motion. He was as comfortable in the cockpit as he was behind the steering wheel of a car—self-assured and in control. The plane rolled down the tarmac, lifted off, and ascended over the industrial area, the old baseball stadium, and the new office buildings that rimmed the Fort Lauderdale airport. We soared above the finger-like canals that define South Florida and then the mile of million-dollar luxury estates and condominiums. Finally, we leveled off, at around 3,500 feet, over a tranquil ocean that looked like a watercolor swirl of marble dunes in every shade of blue and green. The sea was so crystal clear that it seemed as if I could see all the way to the bottom. It was going to be divine to get away from the stress and busyness of work and just relax into a splendid weekend with Roger on "the Rock," the nickname we'd given our contemporary home that jutted out from Cat Island as if presiding over the Atlantic Ocean. Soon, we'd be snuggling up on a chaise lounge on the deck, listening to the surge and splash of the surf, and gazing at the stars. Because there was no commercial electricity on the island, the stars, moon, and galaxies were vivid and brilliant, unlike anything I had ever witnessed.

But I needed to catch up on the latest design industry news. Perhaps there might be a mention of the *Women of Design* exhibition gala that I'd recently helped coordinate. Thirty-three acclaimed female designers from around the nation had created interiors for seven-foot steamer trunks, to express their

The "Rock," our house on Cat Island

design philosophy and ideas. The exhibition celebrated women's outstanding contributions and achievements in architecture and design. In addition, the event had raised $10,000 for cancer research.

Roger glanced at me as he said, "Look up—you're missing a waterspout. There might be a rainbow to follow the shower. Why don't you take a break? You've worked so much overtime this month."

"You're right." I set the magazines aside.

The plane glided between cotton candy clouds and the shadows they cast over the ocean. Roger and I were exactly where we were meant to be. I felt my shoulders relax as the work-week tension melted away. He motioned to the left and said, "See those clouds at eleven o'clock? Do they look like floating dinosaurs to you?"

"Perhaps, a little. What about the cloud at five o'clock? It looks like a gigantic poodle." I kept an eye out for the splendid prismatic double rainbows we'd seen on previous flights but didn't catch sight of any.

Relaxing into the romance of the flight, I remembered the first time I'd flown with Roger. I'd felt much like I imagined Isak Dinesen, author of *Out of Africa*, must have felt at times. With her wayward, adventurous lover, Denys Finch Hatton, she had soared above the spellbinding landscape of Africa and left a fascinating record of what she saw. Being with Roger was like having a comet by the tail.

I reached my hand over and placed it on Roger's thigh. He was twenty years older than me. Sometimes I worried about losing him. I wanted every moment of our life together to count. "We're so lucky to share the love and lifestyle we do. I heard that there are fewer than 220,000 private airplanes in America, and we're sitting in one of them."

He looked at me with an affectionate smile. "And we work long hours to make it happen, don't we?"

"Yes, but it's worth it," I replied as I pressed on his leg, firm enough to remind me that he was strong, fit, and full of boundless energy.

"Will you and Thaniel be repairing the boathouse this weekend?" I asked. Nathaniel, our longtime Bahamian groundskeeper and friend, was helping us remodel two cottages on the thirteen-acre plot.

"I'll talk to him about it while we unload. Hopefully, he had time to catch some conch for us. I want to make conch salad for dinner tonight."

"Ooh." My mouth was already watering. I visualized the conch resting on the ocean floor, connected to a long sailor's rope beside the pier. I was astonished the first time I witnessed the excision of these slimy-looking creatures from the exquisitely sculptured castles they inhabit. Years before, Roger had been part owner of a resort and restaurant on Cat Island. His conch salad had achieved legendary status.

I tilted forward when I caught sight of the island. After Roger turned the plane around the southern tip, I spotted the 2,400-foot airstrip ahead. Most visitors arrive on Cat Island by plane, landing on one of four unmanned airstrips; this one was adjacent to our home at Dolphin Head Point.

Roger said it was like landing on an "ironing board."

Devil's Point was on the right, and the crescent of a shallow bay was to our left. The runway was paved in concrete, flanked by dense brush and tall casuarina pines.

Roger lowered the landing gear. Just minutes stood between us and relaxation in this idyllic setting.

As I glanced at my watch, I touched the spot where my diamond tennis bracelet had been.

It was four thirty—we'd arrive before sunset.

A loud horn blared "beep, beep, beep." It was like the alarm you hear in the hospital when something goes wrong with a monitor.

I looked up at the instrument panel and saw that only two of the three landing gear lights were green, the one for the left and the one for the nose. That meant that if the lights or the lack of an illuminated green light could be trusted, the right main landing gear on my side wasn't in the down-and-locked position.

CHAPTER TWO

Crash on Cat Island

The bow is bent, the arrow flies,
The wingéd shaft of fate.

Ira Aldridge

It all went wrong so quickly.

We could tell something was out of kilter as soon as we touched down along the runway. The airplane tilted to the right. Roger tried immediately to abort the landing. He pressed the throttles fully forward and held them firmly, wide open, calling for as much power as possible to lift us back into the sky. But moving the airplane upward too fast would cause an aerodynamic stall, so Roger retracted the flaps to help the airplane climb. "Come on. *Climb*," he said through gritted teeth. "*Climb*, dammit." His eyes were trained on the line of trees ahead of us, looming ever closer.

With trembling hands, I gripped my seat. I pushed my feet against the floor, bracing for whatever was about to occur. My pulse raced. I felt throbbing in my neck. If we couldn't gain altitude rapidly, we would crash head-on into the hillside in front of us. We were running out of runway. Running out of time. The hillside was just ahead. We weren't high enough.

Roger desperately tried to turn the airplane to the left to avoid the trees. He looked over at me, shocked. Then he seemed to possess an inner realization, and his expression changed to what appeared to me to be deep love, along with something I had never witnessed in him before—fear.

Petrified, I thought, *I'm going to have a heart attack.* The left propeller created an earsplitting shear as it cut through the tops of the trees. The airplane catapulted downward, spiraling out of control. Groceries, suitcases, clothes—everything—spun around the cabin, hitting us. My camera case, heavy with lenses and filters, slammed into the left side of my face. We were a roller coaster gone off its rails, and helplessly trapped. Up became down as the plane spiraled more than one hundred feet before it crash-landed and skidded, ripping and crushing everything in its way. Metal bent and scraped, shrill and deafening.

Then the horror came to a stop.

I experienced the sensation of "coming to," as if I had fainted—dazed and shocked by the reality that I was alive. The seat to my left was empty. I ripped off my seat belt and, finding that I could move, climbed over into Roger's seat.

Roger called up to me from the ground below. Fire surrounded us on every side. "Jump!" he yelled. His arms were up. "I'll catch you."

There was no longer a wing to step down onto. Cargo had shifted during the crash and blocked the exit. I'd have to move fast, before the fire reached the plane. I jumped down some five feet and fell hard onto the ground. Roger helped me to stand up, and we desperately looked around to figure out where to go. We were disoriented; flames blocked our vision. We weren't sure which way would lead us back to the runway.

"We've got to get away from this plane!" Roger said. That's when we heard the voices of children in the distance. He reached for my arm. "Come this way."

The fire raged everywhere. Adrenaline raced through my veins, unstoppable and electrifying. It drove me on—but we met a formidable obstacle.

A wall of dense scrub stood between us and the runway, where the kids must be playing. The crackle grew louder as the fire tore through the brush.

"The fire!" I cried out. "It's spreading everywhere." The heat seared my throat, eyes, and nostrils.

"Hurry!" Roger said. I squinted against the smoke and the sulfuric stench as we worked our way through the unrelenting tangle of brush. Fierce flames raced after us and overtook the dense, thorny underbrush. We were trapped. Roger struggled to press back the obstructing vegetation so I could pass through and escape.

We had gotten about thirty feet from the plane's cabin when a blast propelled me to the ground on my stomach. My back felt liquefied by heat, as if someone had thrown a vat of boiling oil on me. A horrific scream tore from my gut and up through my throat.

"Roger! Roger, where are you? I can't see you. Help me. Oh God, help me!" I struggled to my feet. I had lost all sense of direction and my sight, but I could still hear. Then, in the distance, I heard the voices of the Bahamian children. In despair, I called out to them, "Please keep talking so I can hear you, so I know which direction to go. Please!" I didn't dare cry or stop. My life depended on finding those children.

Despite my anguish, I fought to escape the fire, forcing my way through the thick undergrowth toward the cries of the children. Thorns ripped through my burned flesh. Finally, by the grace of God, I pressed through the last thicket and stumbled out onto the paved runway. Stooped over the tarmac,

Roger was still and silent but alive. I was relieved but wondered how we had become separated. Had he lost sight of me after the explosion, or had he assumed I was dead?

Suddenly I realized that my skin and clothing were still on fire. I dropped to the ground and rolled, over and over, to extinguish the flames. I was unaware of time or space. Sand went deep into my seared flesh and open wounds. I staggered to my feet and yelled out to the children, who looked on in disbelief from about five feet away. "Find Nathaniel. Please! Run as fast as you can!"

Nathaniel was likely waiting for us at the Rock, some three-quarters of a mile away up a dirt-and-gravel road. The children looked at me, stunned. My clothing was scorched, my skin a raw, charred, oozing organ. I must have seemed more demon to them than woman. But we had to get medical attention—*immediately*. So from the depths of my being, I commanded their help. "Go!"

The children took off, and I could only hope they were doing as I'd instructed. I paced back and forth, adrenaline rushing through my exposed veins. Waiting. *Come, Nathaniel.* Wondering what to do next. *Come, Nathaniel.* Across the runway, Roger already seemed to be in shock. If we didn't get medical care right away, we'd die.

I didn't know why—self-preservation maybe—but I felt anger toward him and didn't want to be near him. He gazed blankly into space as if he was unaware of what was happening. If only we'd had a little more runway. If only we'd had a few more minutes to escape the thicket. *If only.* Now, our fate appeared too dreadful to contemplate.

Finally, finally, Nathaniel arrived in his truck.

Horrified by my injuries, he walked over to me. I backed away, shrieking, "Don't touch me, don't touch me!"

Somehow, I recovered rational awareness so I could give him instructions. "Take us to Hawk's Nest. Please." This semi-resort had a marina but, most importantly, an airstrip. We would not survive here. We needed to find someone to fly us back to the States.

I felt like I was choking. My throat was parched. I shouted to the children, who were standing in wide-eyed silence. "Thirsty, can't swallow. Can you run back to the house? There are Cokes in the fridge."

Two of them turned and dashed toward the house. I paced back and forth continuously for about fifteen minutes, trying to find some saliva to swallow. Knowing that if I stopped moving, I'd never be able to move again. Roger was now slumped over on the other side of the runway. I watched for the children and longed to see them return in my direction.

At last, they were in sight. A young boy handed the Coke to me, and I drank it down. It cooled my parched throat. Then Nathaniel guided me to the truck's passenger side and helped me climb in. The tops of my hands were charred, but my palms were intact. The fire had severely burned the inner and outer sides of both of my arms and legs. My tank top, leather belt, short shorts, socks, and sneakers had protected about a third of my body. My bottom, not burned, was the only part that could tolerate touching the truck's seat.

I heard more than saw Nathaniel help Roger into the truck's bed. I couldn't bear to move. I only wanted it to stop hurting. The tailgate slammed. Nathaniel jumped inside and sped up the dirt road and onto the paved two-lane road leading to Hawk's Nest. The tossing and bumping as we traveled delivered a constant stream of unimaginable torture. Every vibration jarred my injured skin and rubbed against raw nerve endings.

Nathaniel radioed for help on his VHF marine-band radio, the system used for most communication on the island. "This is Nathaniel," he said, his usually strong voice shaking. "There's been an accident. Roger's plane crashed, and he and Charlene are badly burned. Can someone fly them to Miami?"

"Where are you?" I recognized the voice of our dear friend Jack Kihm, an orthopedic surgeon who was also a pilot. *Thank God. Thank God.*

"About thirty minutes from Hawk's Nest," Nathaniel said.

Every word tethered me to reality—to life—even as the pain and heat drove deep into my bones. I sat with my bottom on only about four inches of the front seat, with no other part of my back or body touching anything. Maintaining my precarious balance kept even more pain at bay. I held up my arms in the air as if under arrest, palms facing out, and gritted my teeth against the way vibrations from the road were tugging at me. With the minimal energy left after maintaining my posture, I created a mental barrier against four words: *I'm going to die.*

Driving fast but cautiously, Nathaniel's fingers gripped and wrenched and tapped at the wheel. Roger had been like a father to him. A few months ago, Roger had arranged for Nathaniel to get the truck we were riding in. Roger taught Nathaniel how to maintain his vehicle and other equipment, manage his fishing and diving business, and build a house. Now, our lives depended on him.

As dusk descended, we passed by meager cinder-block homes and mile after mile of dense, green landscape. With no roadside lights on the island, we drove through the seemingly endless dark.

I stayed in the same position for thirty long and tormenting minutes until we arrived at Hawk's Nest. Yet our journey had only begun. We'd still have to fly more than two hours to Miami. I couldn't think of hours or minutes when each breath was an ordeal.

A crowd had assembled, and I saw some people holding sheets, buckets of ice, and bottles of water. When we climbed out of the truck to board the airplane that would take us to Miami, onlookers—primarily people we knew—gasped in horror.

Jack Kihm and his friend Bill Skellenger, an Air Force flight surgeon, rushed over to us. Jack asked, "Are either of you having any difficulty breathing?"

"No," we both responded. However, Jack's grim expression showed that he was seriously concerned about our injuries.

"Please don't touch me anywhere," I pleaded. The island's only medical doctor, Dr. Tann, was there but decided to remain on the island since Jack and Bill wanted to accompany us on the flight to Miami. Bill followed me up the stairs into the airplane. I attempted to sit in one of the four seats, but my seared skin couldn't tolerate the feeling of the upholstery.

"I think I'd be better just sitting on the floor," I said and adjusted myself on the reflective windshield visor that Bill had put down. I propped up my legs so they didn't touch the floor.

I was unaware that my facial features had melted and my hair was burned.

Jack then assisted Roger onto the plane. He also preferred the floor. His face was bright red and becoming very swollen and blistered. As Jack cautiously removed the gold chain around Roger's neck, he said, "Buddy, I'm going to hang on to this for you for now." Roger nodded his approval and moaned in pain. I wished I could do something to help him.

I loved him but wondered why he had left me on the plane after the crash. Perhaps because I was unconscious, he thought I was dead. Yet, when I regained consciousness, he was outside of the plane, shouting for me to jump. My mind churned while trying to make sense of this bewildering situation.

As our pilots, Robby Brady and André Dussault, prepared to take off, Roger uttered his first words to me.

"I just paid twenty-five hundred bucks to fix the landing gear."

He knew what had gone wrong—that, once again, the airplane mechanics must have failed to repair the landing gear properly. He had seen what was coming and had kept the horror to himself.

CHAPTER THREE

Flight for Life

To live is to suffer, to survive is to find meaning in the suffering.

Gordon W. Allport

Robby and André piloted our flight for life in a twin-engine Piper Navajo. Jack and Bill gently draped us in clean sheets cut into strips for dressings to cover our wounded areas in an almost vain attempt to keep us clean and reduce exposure to the air. They did this to lessen the pain.

"I'm not going to make it," I whispered against the discomfort in my throat. "I feel like I'm going to die. The pain . . . it's unbearable."

"Are you allergic to any medications?" Jack said.

"Codeine," I replied.

Then Jack turned to Roger and asked, "How about you? Do you know of any allergies?"

Roger responded in a strained voice. "Nothing I'm aware of."

Jack reached for a syringe in his kit and filled it with seventy-five milligrams of nirvana in the form of Demerol. Within moments of receiving the injection, I felt less anxious and less aware of the pain. Roger appeared to be getting some relief as well. His body wasn't as tense, and his moans were less frequent. But his face continued to swell.

I overheard a conversation between Jack and Robby about the need to refuel.

Jack's voice: "Do we have enough fuel to make it to Miami?"

Robby: "I think so."

Jack: "That's not good enough. Nassau is our last chance to refuel. We're going to have to land."

I couldn't believe what I had just heard. Stopping would delay our arrival time by at least another thirty minutes. "Are you sure we can't make it without stopping?"

Jack turned around as if surprised I could still form thoughts. Or speak. "Running out of fuel over the ocean would . . . not help you," Jack said.

It would kill us all, he meant to say. But the delay might kill Roger and me. I'd heard stories of seriously injured people who died in Nassau hospitals. "Don't leave us in Nassau. No matter what happens. We have to get to Miami."

I could barely see Robby's profile against the night sky outside the cockpit windshield. Everywhere, there was blackness. As if death enveloped us.

Jack attended to Roger, who was wincing in pain. His skin was red and blistered as if grotesquely sunburned. Rarely had I ever seen Roger in pain. He looked into my eyes but didn't say a word. I'd met him in a bar by chance and had fallen for him after one night together. Shortly after that, we were inseparable. But now, this adventurous man I'd hoped to marry was becoming unrecognizable.

I had no indication of how repulsive I must have appeared. Although my extensive bodily burns were visible to me, I didn't realize the fire had burned my face. It made me feel sick to my stomach to think that I might be a mirror of Roger's appearance and suffering.

The plane descended and—*thank God*—touched down lightly. A sigh of relief. We taxied to the apron and turned away from the terminal to refuel. Angry customs officials met us. "Why are you flying after dark?" one demanded.

Robby said, "We have an emergency and need fuel. We must leave as soon as possible."

"We can't do this," the irritated agent responded. Outside the cabin exit, I could see him pacing in annoyance.

"Come over here," Jack told him. "We have a medical emergency."

The agent stuck his head into the plane, saw us, and appeared overcome by the putrid smell of charred flesh and our shocking appearance. He squinted his eyes, clenched his jaw—then backed away. "How much gas do you need?"

Jack and Bill provided customs with our names and ages. The agents stopped short of demanding identification from our two pilots and our ad hoc, lifesaving medical crew.

The customs agent did order Robby to file a flight plan. He exited the plane and briskly walked into the airport to take care of it.

Unfortunately, the agents requested the wrong type of fuel. It took an almost unbearable twenty minutes to locate the correct fuel truck. I couldn't believe the agents could have made such a mistake.

Hold on. Stay focused. Make it to Miami. Miami. Make it to Miami.

*

When I once again heard a truck engine arriving, I knew the fuel was flowing into the tanks. I tried not to breathe the toxic gasoline fumes, but it was impossible to avoid them. They made me feel lightheaded and like I was going to vomit.

Twenty more wretched minutes. Jack and Bill paced outside the plane. A fireman handed Jack a container of ice that he used to dribble cold water onto our bandages. It was soothing. Robby radioed for permission to take off.

We ascended once again into the black vacuum of nightfall. Destination: Miami International Airport. We were still here. We could still breathe and talk. *Miami. Miami.* Maybe we were going to live.

Shortly after our departure, Jack said to Robby, "Patch us into Miami air traffic control. Ask them to connect us to the Burn Center at Jackson Memorial. We need to talk to a burn doc."

"Air traffic control, this is N2586X," Robby said. "We have a male and female on board who are severely burned. Can you patch us into the Burn Center at Jackson Memorial Hospital to speak with a doctor as soon as possible? This is a life and death situation. Please respond immediately."

It took a few minutes to establish the connection. Since only one headset was on board, Robby repeated everything for Jack and Bill.

"Roger, I'm on it," the air traffic controller responded. "Hold while I connect you."

"Mr. Brady, you can go ahead. I have Dr. Fernandez on the line," said the air traffic controller.

Jack rattled off the facts. "We have a female, age forty-two, and a male, age sixty-three, burned on more than fifty percent of their bodies. Both are conscious and sipping water. They are not in respiratory distress yet."

Yet.

"What are their vital signs?" asked Dr. Fernandez in a calm, smooth voice.

"Charlene's pulse is 120," said Bill. "Roger's is 105. Unfortunately, we don't have a blood pressure cuff."

"Are there any other injuries?"

"They both have minor cuts and scratches but no broken bones. It doesn't appear that there are any spinal or neurological injuries."

"Do you have means of giving oxygen?" asked Dr. Fernandez.

"No, doc, we don't," said Bill.

"Have you covered their burns?"

"Yes, we've used clean sheets."

"Cool the burns, but keep them covered," ordered Dr. Fernandez. "How soon do you expect to arrive?"

"We should land at Miami International in about thirty-five minutes," Bill said.

"We'll start setting up IVs, organizing dressings, and putting staff on alert. Our first concern is their airways. Were the victims trapped inside the airplane?"

"No, they escaped from the plane," said Jack. "We think their burns are from a fuel tank explosion."

"What time did the injuries occur?"

"About four thirty p.m."

"Are the victims oriented? Talking appropriately?"

"Yes, although we've advised them to talk as little as possible. We don't want them to lapse into respiratory arrest," Jack said. "This is no place to perform a tracheotomy."

Anxiety on the rise, my breathing became more like panting as I listened to the conversation. I breathed in deeply and exhaled slowly, trying to calm down. I couldn't imagine the outcome of a surgical procedure performed under such dire conditions.

"Thank you for the advance status report. This will help us prep the OR. Our trauma team will be prepared and waiting for them."

They would be waiting for us. The OR, with its sweet reassurance of anesthesia, would be ready. "Trauma team"—the name felt like an acknowledgment of what we'd been enduring. Even after hearing Jack's devastating description of our injuries, I thought they would know what to do if we could just reach the trauma center.

Both Jack and Bill had training in Advanced Cardiac Life Support and Advanced Trauma and Life Support, which helped them to organize their thinking. Still, they didn't have the supplies to tend to our rapidly deteriorating condition.

Aware of my charred skin, I sensed the uncertainty wafting through the air. No one felt sure we would make it. All I could do was sit there, maintaining my balance, and wait.

To keep my eyes open, though, was to see this jolting version of my fiancé, whose face, neck, arms, hands, and legs were becoming unrecognizable. I sensed my mind shutting down and life draining from my brain—my focus blurring. Then violent shaking as shock set in.

My mind drifted, only focusing again when I sipped water that teased an insatiable thirst.

For three and a half tortured hours, during which I clung to consciousness by a fragile silk filament, Roger had spoken only one sentence to me. I'd said nothing in return. Would our magical life together end in deadly silence?

I prayed to God: *Please don't let us die. Please help us to reach the hospital. Please let my sister and mom know how deeply I cherish and love them and that I will always be with them. Please forgive me for my many sins. Please give me the strength to survive. I don't want to die!*

Quickly, I turned my thoughts back to surviving so as not to cry and become more anxious and distraught. Took another deep breath. Tried to be quiet and still, as Jack had suggested.

Finally, Miami. Our plane was cleared immediately to land and told to taxi to customs at General Aviation. With disbelief and shock bordering on rage, I learned that communication had dropped within the bowels of the near-empty airport. No ambulance awaited us.

"What the hell do you mean you didn't know anything about our emergency?" Jack yelled into the radio. "We've been talking with air traffic control since we left Rock Sound! I suggest you immediately get a fucking ambulance here, unless you want to be responsible for these people dying."

The silk filament connecting me to life frayed with the sudden halt in forward movement. Time stood still in the cabin of the plane. Tears welled in my eyes, and I feared their salt on my ravaged skin. I couldn't take much more. Where were our saviors?

Minutes ticked away. My anxiety surged again. My heartbeat pulsed in my veins. My disappointment turned into rage as my eyes followed every movement of our crew, taking out their frustration on officials outside the aircraft. After all their efforts, had we persevered through interminable time and distance to die here on the tarmac at Miami International Airport?

In the distance, I thought I heard the piercing sound of sirens. My eyes opened wide. I strained to listen. Then—*thank God*—those glorious flashing lights that said someone recognized our plight.

The incredible will to live and the survival instinct that had sustained me were replenished with a flood of relief when I saw the ambulances. These were people who understood the nature of an emergency.

The paramedics assisted Roger out of the plane. I scooted down the steps on my bottom. I was amazed that we could both stand and walk. The gurney in front of me, draped in white linens, was the finish line in a perverse marathon. I had made it alive. The paramedics helped me to crawl onto the stretcher and covered me with a sheet except for my arms, which remained outstretched in the same position. The paramedics were skilled and compassionate. The female medic asked me, "Who is your nearest relative?"

I responded with Melissa's name, phone number, and location in Wilmington, North Carolina.

The paramedics lifted the stretcher into the ambulance. In front of me, I could see other medics assisting a swollen, frightened, and stunned Roger onto a stretcher and into an ambulance. I never took my eyes off him until the ambulance doors closed and I could no longer see him.

Inside the ambulance, the female medic said, "I'm going to start an IV so we can give you something for the pain. Are you allergic to any drugs?"

"Codeine."

"It may hurt a little when I insert the needle." I thought I couldn't stand any more pain, but I'd take the prick to get some relief. She filled a syringe and injected the contents into the IV line. Rigid muscles relaxed, and the tension that had held me together for the last six hours unwound.

Finally, in the ambulance, I could let go.

CHAPTER FOUR

Morphine Memories

The real test of a man is not how well he plays the role he has invented for himself, but how well he plays the role that destiny assigned to him.

Jan Patocka

Morphine drips into my bloodstream, kidnapping my mind and sending me on a terrifying ride—I'm trapped in a trance.

Am I going to die?

Horse hooves pound and carriage wheels rattle on cobblestone streets. Yes, I can see it ahead—a coach with two lit lanterns glowing along its sides. It's darting too fast through the narrow streets. In the dim light, I can see two magnificent black stallions pulling the carriage just before disappearing into the fog.

I'm so hot.

Red flames flare from torches positioned next to two guards dressed in black shrouds. They hold pitchforks between hands covered by black gloves. In the dungeon, a satanic entity sits on a giant medieval chair. Clad in a long black cape and tunic, with a hood covering his head, he reveals little, but I see his scorching eyes in a jagged lightning flash. This fiendish creature with his haunting countenance sits in silence.

When my eyes meet his, I am swept into a tumultuous, spinning vortex that swirls me deeper and deeper into its bottomless pit of hot, black waters. Drowning. Smothering. Unable to breathe. There is no escape. Pain, fear, and suffering infuse me. I am only energy, yet with senses intact to witness the unimaginable.

Please—if I live—will I heal?

I'm at Cat Island, sort of. This island connects to another island unfamiliar to me. To cross over to the other island, slender Bahamian men, women, and children dressed in fatigues must walk across an enormous rock formation resembling the moon's craterlike surface. Nathaniel is among them, near the middle of the rock. Dark clouds roll in, and a windy storm pummels the island. Jagged bolts of lightning tear through the sky; thunder roars. The tide swells with the raging winds, causing waves to crash against the rocks, splashing onto my hot skin. The islanders flee, pushing and shoving one another. The rock crumbles into the sea, bringing screaming men and women with it. Where is Nathaniel? Did he drown in the island disaster?

Will Roger still want to marry me?

It's snowing as my fiancé and I sit in a cozy Manhattan bistro, talking and laughing with friends at a table covered in a red-and-white-checkered cloth. The year is 1910, and the air is filled with holiday scents: evergreens, candle wax, cranberries, and coffee. Suddenly I'm sitting in a wheelchair, listening in helpless disbelief as my fiancé's sister tries to convince him to not marry me. She says that I will be an enormous burden. He frowns and rejects her warnings, and soon I'm standing with crutches as we marry in a private ceremony. I wear a delicate white lace dress with a scalloped neckline, and my silky auburn hair is pinned in the style of a geisha, with soft strands resting on my cheeks. My fiancé wears tiny gold wire-rimmed glasses, a black silk suit, a crisp white dress shirt, and a bow tie. I can see that he deeply loves me.

The scene shifts. I look around and see my husband in his office at our home. He is gathering his things. I'm confused. Is he leaving? Where is he going? Why is he going? My eyes fill with tears as I call out to him, "Please tell me what's wrong?"

Did anyone call my sister? I want Melissa to have my diamond bracelet.

Our cozy, art-filled home has many large windows, and embers glow from a fire in the grate. Bookshelves hold hundreds of thin, square paper packages with red-and-blue print.

"Over there, over there," I say to Melissa, sitting in the chair next to my bed. "Take some money if you need it. See, it's there in those thin white packages on the shelf."

But Melissa can't find the money. I don't understand. I can see the packages of money there on the middle shelf of the bookcase next to my bed. If only I could move, I could get them for her, but we seem to be at an impasse: she can't see them, and I can't hand them to her.

I'm so thirsty. Can I have something to drink?

Around the ceiling in my room, a hippie-looking, olive-complected man races a psychedelic orange-and-flamingo-pink motorcycle. Vroom! Vroom! The engine roars, and I feel a breeze against my face as the bike speeds by. Sometimes the bike moves through an arc of slow motion; at other times, it zooms by, leaving sparks. Now I see it outdoors, racing through the streets of neighborhoods. A skinny man dressed in white scrubs, with a mustache and thick hair the color of black ink, rides as if the bike were a bronco. Circling the room, round, frightful faces without bodies bounce about, scaring me.

Where is Roger?

Wrapped like a mummy in white bandages with only my eyes visible. Tubes connected to monitoring devices protrude from my nose and mouth like arteries attached to the heart. Nurses dressed in white blouses and skirts roll my body into a sanctuary filled with mourners. It is so vivid: the long red carpet lined with artificial palm trees, the pulpit shaped like the bow of a boat. The somber mood lingers in the air, like dense fog hanging over a still lake. Now there is a lake and a rowboat. Roger is asleep in it.

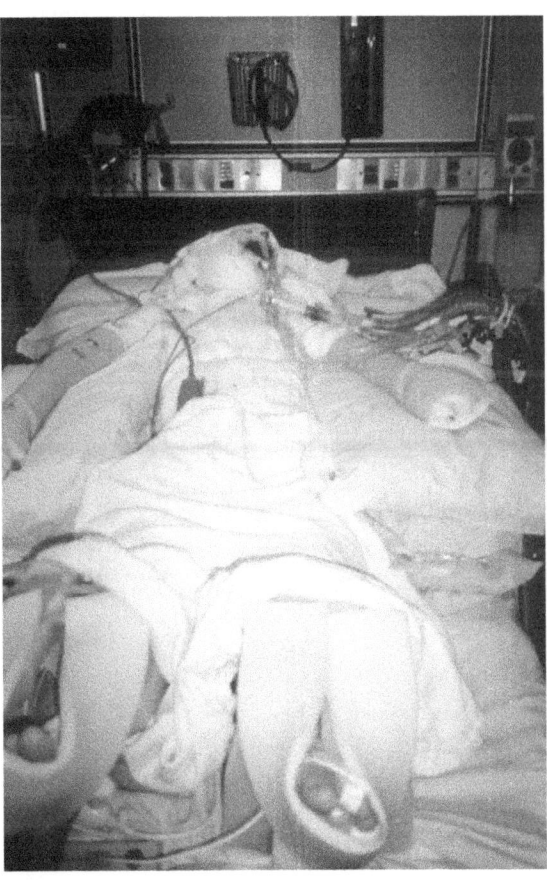

Morphine-induced coma

*

Is someone there?

There was light and sound in my room, and I could see Melissa at the foot of my bed. She was painting my toenails.

"Oh my God, you're awake! Blink your eyes if you can hear me."

I blinked and she smiled in elation.

My sister. They'd found Melissa, and she was there.

And I was there, too. I blinked and blinked and blinked. I had survived.

Later, I learned that morphine had caused the bizarre and terrifying hallucinations.

"The doctors told us you couldn't live through such excruciating pain without the morphine," Melissa said.

I had been in a drug-induced coma for sixty-one days at the University of Miami's Jackson Memorial Hospital Burn Center. Throughout that time, I existed in this mysterious holding place between the living and the dead—limbo.

For fifteen minutes, four times a day—and only on good days, when I wasn't writhing or thrashing—Mom and Melissa were allowed to be with me. They had to scrub with disinfectant soap and don a sterile white paper apron, mask, and gown and a hat that looked like a blue pizza-chef hat. Day after day, they repeated this ritual and visited just to savor a few minutes with me.

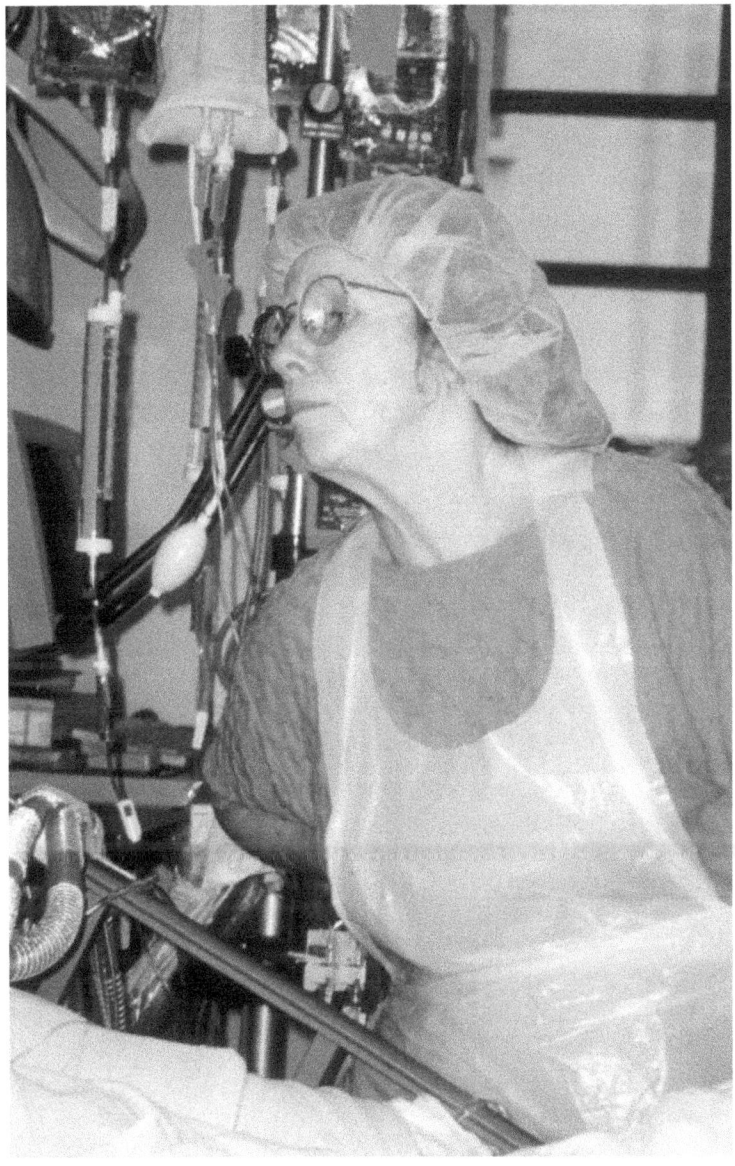

Mom caring for me in the ICU

Sterile white gauze covered my body. An endotracheal
tube protruded from my chest like a vacuum hose, delivering

medicine or removing bodily fluids. The ventilator and tracheostomy tube prevented me from speaking or screaming. I felt hot and thirsty, as if I were in an incubator. My head arched back, and my mouth was locked wide open as if I were screaming. Mom said that my flesh looked like "raw meat."

After regaining full consciousness, I saw the thin white packages that Melissa couldn't see. The packages contained sterile gauze pads for dressing changes, not money. And much to my surprise, the olive-complected man with dark hair and mustache was my occupational therapist. The frightful faces that bounced around the ceiling were helium balloons from friends meant to cheer me.

Just as Dorothy, Toto, and their companions traipsed through the poppies until they were overcome by sleep, morphine had transported me to a foreign place where I'd met different characters who accompanied me on my journey back to my mom, my sister, and reality.

Yet, unlike Dorothy, there was no return home to salve my broken heart.

CHAPTER FIVE

Rehab and More Rehab

The best thing about the future is that it comes only one day at a time.

Abraham Lincoln

Three months after the crash

As the paramedics pushed my gurney through the stark white corridors of the burn unit toward the elevator, I trembled. I was leaving the protection of the Burn Center to enter an unknown facility staffed with strangers. Would my new caregivers be as competent and compassionate as those who had cared for me at the Burn Center? I had grown attached to my doctors, nurses, and therapists at Jackson Memorial Hospital. Leaving them was like leaving a safe shelter during a storm. Dr. Gillon Ward, the burn unit's resolute and formidable medical director, came over to me. He rested his hand on my shoulder and said, "You've made remarkable progress. We'll see you in the clinic in a few weeks." He smiled and extended his hand in farewell to Mom and Melissa.

To his surprise, they reached out and hugged him. His expression softened and grew more endearing. Dr. Ward wasn't a "huggable" kind of physician—he was stern and serious. I sensed how happy he was to see me cross this threshold, returning to the world of the living. I was told that there were days when he imagined I would leave as a corpse, another statistic of a fatal burn injury.

As I left behind the kindhearted caregivers whom I trusted, tears welled in my eyes and rolled down my cheeks, reaching my chin. As far as I'd come, I couldn't raise my arm to dry them myself. Melissa wiped my face. "Don't cry. Everything is going to be okay. We'll be behind the ambulance, with you all the way."

The elevator descended to the ground level. The automatic doors opened, and the male attendants rolled my stretcher outside into the bright sunshine. The glare was blinding. The attendants lifted the stretcher into the ambulance and locked it into place. "Could you please raise my head so I can see my mom and sister in the car behind?"

One of them obliged and made the adjustment. Through the tiny square windows in the ambulance's back doors, I could see the fronds of palm trees against the blue sky. Bedridden in my room in the burn unit, I had only been able to see the sky.

During the drive, I kept my eyes on Mom and Melissa, as she drove my car, following close behind the ambulance. They were my umbilical cord, essential to my very survival. I strained to keep my eyes on them during the uncomfortably bumpy, hour-long ride to the rehab hospital.

The ambulance pulled into the parking area under the portico of HealthSouth Sunrise Rehabilitation Hospital, a long, sprawling, yellow, one-story building with a tile roof. The attendants lifted my stretcher and placed it on the ground. They then maneuvered the gurney through the automatic glass doors, into the sunlit reception area, and down bustling hallways to room 105.

The small, square room adjacent to the busy nurses' station was not as institutional as my room had been at the burn unit. It had a blue chair, a small pine dresser, a blue leather reclining chair, and a bathroom. I also noted the marble ledge under the window where Melissa carefully placed treasured photographs of Roger and me, along with mementos from friends and family. In addition, she taped a collection of cards from family, friends, and associates to the walls. Best of all, the large window that overlooked the lawn outside my room was at my eye level. For the first time in three months, I could see breeze-caressed palm trees, ruffled pink hibiscus blooms, and graceful birds in flight framed by soft clouds.

A petite, middle-aged, Filipina woman with a shiny, dark pageboy haircut smiled as she entered the room. "Hello, welcome to HealthSouth," she said. "I'm Marilyn. I'll be your primary nurse. We've been preparing for your arrival. Once you get settled in, let me know if you have any questions. I'll be on duty until eleven o'clock."

She handed Melissa a paper and said, "Here's the menu for dinner and breakfast. Just circle what she wants to eat, and I'll take the form to the cafeteria since the aide has already collected the forms for this evening."

"Oh, thanks," Melissa responded. "I'd like to walk with you to see where the cafeteria is. My sister is a great cook and very selective about what she eats."

Melissa described my choices for dinner and circled my selections, since I couldn't read the words due to the jam-like salve in my right eye. This was a welcome change from the burn unit, where I had been fed intravenously and through a feeding tube until just a few days before my discharge. The feeding tube port still protruded from my abdomen, resembling a freshly cut watermelon's pink, moist texture. Melissa had told me the decision to insert a feeding tube most likely helped save my life. However, it was one of the most upsetting and distressing choices Mom had to make.

Marilyn returned to the room and assured me they had all my records from Jackson Memorial. But there was no assuring me of anything. Whenever she came near me, my pulse raced, and my eyes followed her every move. When she reached over to touch me, I tried to pull away—she looked just like one of the evil women in my hallucinations. It didn't make sense. One minute, she appeared to me to be caring. The next minute, she looked threatening. She approached me with a pill and said, "Take this. It will help you sleep." But I thought she was trying to poison me.

"Should I take this? Is it just to help me sleep?" I cried out to Melissa. My thoughts were as incongruent and distorted as fusion jazz—irrational, even, but quite sensible to me. Unknowingly, I was in the preliminary stages of withdrawal from morphine, which can cause paranoid delusions. No one had prepared me for this—or, if someone had told me about the symptoms, I definitely didn't remember.

"Have you ever cared for a burn survivor before?" I asked Marilyn.

"Yes, I've been assigned to be your primary nurse because of my experience treating burn victims."

I was uncomfortable with the word "victim."

"In the morning," Marilyn continued, "your physiatrist will be here to meet you. His name is Dr. Sassoon. You'll like him. He has a great bedside manner, and he's very kind."

"What's a physiatrist?" Never had I heard of this kind of physician.

"It's a doctor who specializes in rehabilitation."

I felt like I was in a foreign country, and I didn't speak the language. I wasn't familiar with the jargon of rehabilitation and burn care. I needed to learn to play a more active role in my recovery. My new circumstances reminded me of my first days at a variety of new jobs. Those days were my least favorite because I didn't like being the one with only the slightest knowledge of what was happening and what was expected. Usually, I'm the person who plans everything, develops the strategies, organizes the activities, gathers the information and data, and directs the events. At the Design Center of the Americas (DCOTA), I had directed staff in all sorts of tasks, including producing major conferences, selecting and booking acclaimed guest speakers, arranging catering and entertainment, promotion, and advertising. On the day of the accident, I had overseen a gathering of prominent dignitaries and businesspeople for a luncheon fundraiser for gubernatorial candidate Jeb Bush. Former president George H. W. Bush and Barbara Bush had been there. I'd gone from being vice president of communications at the top design center in America to someone who didn't even have the vocabulary to understand her current situation.

After dinner, I struggled to concentrate. When Mom and Melissa spoke, it was as if I was watching a silent movie. I saw their lips move and their expressions change, but I didn't process the conversation. Agitated and tired, I tried to shift my position, to be more comfortable, but I couldn't move without assistance. I wondered about what would happen next. How would Dr. Sassoon orchestrate reviving my atrophied muscles and weak, nonfunctioning limbs? I felt like a puppet collapsed in a child's room, waiting for someone to pick up the pieces and pull the strings so that I could speak, walk, sit, stand, and dance. I'd been told that, the next day, various health care workers would poke, prod, and manipulate my body to help me regain strength, better speech, and mobility.

On weekdays during junior high school, I had volunteered to assist with "ranging" a young girl with muscular dystrophy. Three other volunteers and I would surround the large table where the adolescent girl was lying. Simultaneously, we moved her arms and legs in a coordinated motion, to sustain muscle tone and neurological pathways. *Was it possible the therapists might perform this type of exercise on me?*

Unsuccessfully, I tried to put all the questions and anxiety aside so I could sleep. I looked over at Mom as she yawned and saw that Melissa was straining to stay awake. "Try to go to sleep," Melissa whispered. "You're right beside the nurses' station. They'll keep a close eye on you. Try to relax and close your eyes."

"You and Mom look exhausted, but I don't want you to leave me here with these strangers. I don't feel safe."

"We'll ask if we can spend the night," Melissa said.

There weren't any accommodations for family members to stay in patient rooms. My room had only one blue recliner, which didn't look very comfortable. Marilyn permitted Melissa and Mom to linger a bit longer after visiting hours. When they finally had to leave and the lights were turned out, frightening shadows bounced off the walls of my room. Patients down the hall moaned in pain. Out of the corner of my eye, I saw strangers passing by my doorway. My pulse raced; I clenched my teeth. My body stiffened in fear. I took deep breaths and exhaled slowly to calm down.

Marilyn came in to say good night. "Please, can you get a lamp?" I was scared, alone there in the dark.

"I'll see what I can do, but it may be tomorrow before I can requisition one. You don't have to worry. Someone will be checking on you throughout the night. Now, try to get some rest."

Near midnight, Marilyn entered my room carrying a pink ginger jar lamp with a fluted shade. With the light on, I felt a sense of security. The warm glow softened the hospital room and made it more like home. Content, I surrendered to my new environment and drifted to sleep.

During the next few days, my thoughts fluctuated from

rational to irrational without warning. "Did I experience a head injury, or is something wrong with my mind?" I asked Robin, an exceptionally competent, caring nurse. "My thoughts are all mixed up. I feel like people are trying to kill me; it's insane." "It's probably the morphine." "Morphine? I don't want to be on morphine. Take me off it. I'm not going to take any more!"

Concerned, Robin said, "You'll have to talk to Dr. Sassoon about this. We must follow the orders on your chart. I'll call him for you, okay?"

A few minutes later, Robin held the phone to my ear so I could talk to Dr. Sassoon. "The only thing that I have left is my mind. So, please, take me off any mind-altering drugs. I want to think clearly, to comprehend and process information, so I can know what is happening to me and what I need to do to improve."

"I understand." His voice was calming. "But I can't just stop the morphine all at once. You must be weaned from it gradually. So, we'll expedite the process as much as possible."

Dr. Sassoon was soft-spoken and attentive. I sensed that he was deeply affected by my extensive injuries. He assembled a team of specialists to monitor all aspects of my rehabilitation, including a pulmonary doctor, a gastroenterologist, occupational and physical therapists, speech and recreational therapists, a nutritionist, and a psychologist.

I continued to think that different people were plotting to kill me. Finally, one night, I was sure I was dying. On that occasion, about twenty caregivers surrounded me, and I believed they were gathered in my room for a death watch. "Please don't cremate me. I thought I wanted to be cremated, but not anymore." I didn't hear their response or if they even made one and was catapulted into a higher degree of paranoia.

Alarmed, I reached for the call button, but I couldn't move my fingers. I tried calling out but couldn't speak.

This scenario played out over and over for days. Withdrawal from morphine was wicked; I was filled with terror, paranoia, and rampant anxiety.

I couldn't eat without help. I couldn't use a telephone. Unable to sit up by myself or use my arms, I depended on others for every need. I was afraid to be left alone, concerned that I would be unable to obtain assistance to use the bedpan or to call for help. Finally, I asked Melissa to hire an aide to sit with me through the scary, long, and lonely nights.

Melissa and Mom recruited Joyce, a nurse from Jamaica, to be with me overnight until I could sleep without terrifying nightmares and could push the call button for assistance. Joyce had a furrowed brow, and her facial expression reflected years of strife. She reminded me of Carrie Mae, the tall, slender Black woman who had cared for me as a child while my mother was at work. Like Carrie Mae, there was a tender gentleness about Joyce. She was calm, attentive, and responsive to my questions and requests. The first night she reported to my room, she exclaimed, "Oh, my dear, you have survived quite a lot, haven't you? God must have something significant for you to do, to have spared you." She watched over me like a cat stalking a blue jay. I felt safe with her sitting across from me. Sometimes, when I couldn't sleep, we talked. Joyce had high blood pressure and was not a stranger to illness. She had several grandchildren but lived alone. We chatted about Jamaica, an island I had visited on my first honeymoon. At night, Joyce would find snacks for me and often produced the cup of juice that her sparkling eyes told me she knew I'd like. Nightly, I anticipated her arrival and began to feel more at ease in my new surroundings.

I hated for anyone to close the door to my private room. With the door closed, I felt trapped and claustrophobic. During fire drills, the door had to be shut. Whenever this occurred, my anxiety soared. I was terrified of being in another fire. The flames. The searing pain. Whenever I started to tumble into these dark moods, I tried to find hope in the image that Melissa had created for me: I would walk again one day. To allay my panic, I focused on the day I would once again be self-sufficient.

Night after night, nightmares cornered me inside burning rooms. I'd wake up with my heart pounding as if it was going to explode from my chest. It would take a few seconds to reconnect with reality and realize I had had a bad dream.

My beloved, camel-colored, corduroy teddy bear, "Hot Teddy," was constantly close so that I could see his smiling button eyes. His expressive, magical face cheered and comforted me through the tormenting days and nights. Weeks later, when I could hold a modified pen, the first picture that I drew was of Hot Teddy and the pink ginger jar lamp.

Once I could write, I began to chart my therapy schedule and daily activities of physical therapy, speech therapy, occupational therapy, and meetings with Dr. Mic, my psychologist. The first chart looked like a toddler had scribbled it, but it helped me plan and organize my days. Documenting my schedule gave me a sense of control in my rehabilitation, which was a small source of relief. I so needed something to be within my control.

Left: The soft glow of the lamp in the night eased my fear. Right: My drawings of Hot Teddy.

CHAPTER SIX

Funeral Fog

Like a bird out of our hand,
Like a light out of our heart,
You are gone.

H. D. Hymen

Four months after the crash

I awakened feeling a tiny bit stronger, as if I was beginning to make some progress, and my spirits lifted. I knew my condition would improve in time, and I believed I wanted to live, as long as I had my family, faith, friends, and hope.

One morning, Mom entered my room loaded down with clean laundry, mail, and brownies. She began to put the clothes in the chest of drawers. She then handed me an envelope from Misty, Roger's thirteen-year-old granddaughter. The letter jolted my memory and triggered the question that could threaten my existence.

"Where is Roger? Is he here, too?" Mom turned her eyes

away from me. Her bottom lip began to quiver. Then she whispered, "Roger didn't make it, sweetie."

"But I saw him climb onto the stretcher."

Mom could no longer contain her tears. They spilled down her cheeks. "He's . . ." I couldn't mutter the word. I couldn't process the words my mom had spoken. "He's . . . dead?"

My entire body stiffened.

Just a few months ago, I'd been planning to marry Roger at an island wedding. My mind was racing ahead and dwelling on the unfathomable loneliness before me. I sat in wary silence. Mom dabbed at the tears on my cheeks and nose, afraid to hug me because it might hurt instead of help.

When I finally accepted that he was dead, I recalled something odd. "Mom, I know it sounds crazy, but I thought I'd attended his funeral while hospitalized at Jackson Memorial."

"You were still in a coma on the day of his funeral. The doctors advised everyone caring for you not to mention his death until you asked about him."

All this time, while I had been reorienting and gaining more awareness of my situation and surroundings, I'd been living within a protected bubble. "Did he ever regain consciousness?"

"No. His room was across from yours. Melissa visited. She played reggae music for him, but he was heavily medicated and disoriented. His eyes appeared frozen in a state of shock. His burns were less severe than yours."

Separated by a hallway, we had been lost in our own misery, fighting to stay alive.

I leaned on my left arm and tried to shift my weight to face Mom. "Then what happened?"

"His age worked against him. He developed sepsis, and his body couldn't fight the infection. They told us it's a common cause of death for burn survivors."

This news was so hard to take in. Roger was gone. "Were you with him? At the end?"

Tears flooded Mom's eyes as she continued with a broken voice. "His family wouldn't let us visit Roger once they found out we had retained an attorney. They assumed that we believed the crash was Roger's fault."

Mom and Melissa had been by his side every moment that they couldn't be with me, until Roger's children banned them from his room. Mom and Melissa had adored him and were stunned by what they thought was his children's unthinkable behavior. Banning Mom and Melissa from visiting Roger began a nasty conflict between my family and Roger's children. Mom and Melissa shielded me from what they perceived as his children's cruel, unreasonable actions whenever possible.

Likely, Roger's children were worried about their inheritance. They would lose everything if the crash was determined to be Roger's fault. Perhaps their attorney had instructed them to deny Mom and Melissa visitation rights. All Mom knew was that she and Melissa could no longer be with Roger.

And there was more to the story. While I was comatose, Roger's children had mandated that my belongings be removed from the condo where Roger and I had lived together during the last four and a half years. Mom and Melissa were allowed to remove only the items they could prove were mine—a ludicrous task. In addition, Roger's daughter Renee refused to let the movers take the Yamaha piano that Roger had given me. She told Melissa, "The piano is mine. She'll never play again."

I was upset to learn about this situation, but I wasn't surprised by his children's reactions, except for Renee's. She and I had become friends, and I was fond of her adolescent daughter, Misty. Roger's other children lived in Maine and were distant geographically and emotionally.

When Roger and I first fell in love, all his children thought I was a "gold digger," until they recognized how much I loved and cared for their dad. I had encouraged Roger to reconcile his relationship with his estranged sons, who I thought had gravely disappointed him, and he did. All his children blamed him for their circumstances because Roger had divorced their mom to marry another woman long before he met me. The children seemed jealous of the life Roger and I had enjoyed. So it was no surprise to me that they did not seem interested in my well-being or the possibility of splitting any insurance claims on the aircraft or any settlement from legal actions against the manufacturer of the plane, the engines, or the landing gear.

On the other hand, Mom and Melissa managed so many complex and confusing situations with grace and dignity. They had channeled their anger and fear into positive actions like running and walking. They received an outpouring of love, prayers, encouragement, and financial support from Mom's church, Center United Methodist Church in Summerfield, North Carolina. Friends, family, and associates prayed, called, and sent hundreds of cards, dollars, and well-wishes. Melissa's companion of nine years, Ryan, and Mom's companion, Hal, were their anchors in this fierce and unrelenting storm.

Roger's funeral had been at the First Presbyterian Church of Pompano Beach, the "pink church," on NE Twenty-Sixth Avenue. Renee had married Hernando there, and their daughter, Misty, had been baptized at the pink church. Renee must have been shaken by having to reconcile those joyous walks down the red-carpeted aisle with this heartbreaking walk to bid a forever farewell to her beloved "daddy." How ironic that celebrations of life and love should occur in the same place as memorials of death.

Melissa told me the pastor asked the congregation to "pray for Charlene Pell." Still, there was no mention of my relationship with Roger. How could that be? Wasn't I the love of Roger's life? That was how he had consistently introduced me to friends and family members. Frequent references were made to his ex-wife Connie, who sat in the audience with her new husband. All of Roger's closest friends and family knew that he had adored me.

Yet, at the ceremony, it was as if I hadn't existed.

I felt violated and heartbroken. The memorial service had disregarded my significance to Roger.

Jolted by all this disturbing news, I redirected my attention to my own survival. I knew that I couldn't lose my concentration and sink into despair. Otherwise, I, too, might die.

CHAPTER SEVEN

Who Is This Person in the Mirror?

*He who has a why to live for can bear with
almost any how.*

Friedrich Nietzsche

Four months after the crash

Finding a mirror in a burn unit was like finding a four-leaf clover. While the startled, uneasy expressions on the faces of people who met me for the first time had clued me in to the fact that something was disturbing about my face, my distorted reflection in a silver spoon provided the first glimpse of what they saw.

After I arrived at the rehab hospital, I asked for a mirror. The nurse's furrowed brow alerted me that I should prepare to be shocked. The nurse retrieved a mirror and handed it to Melissa so she could be by my side when I looked. Melissa leaned over my shoulder as she held the mirror so I could see myself. The only features of the person in the mirror that resembled me were my hazel eyes. My eyebrows were missing.

My skin was a screaming red, with raised seams where skin grafts had been stitched together to cover raw tissue. Scar bands encircled my mouth, which now appeared tiny. My lower lip protruded out and down. My right earlobe was gone, and the left one looked like it had melted. Little sprigs of red hair jutted out of my wounded, red scalp. My chin appeared to be pulled down to my neck, as if part of my neck was missing.

My sister, Melissa, with me the first time I looked into a mirror to see myself after the accident

I sat silent, stunned, while tears rolled down my cheeks.
I looked like an alien.
"You won't always look like this," Melissa said. "In a few

months, when your wounds have healed, you can begin to have plastic surgery. But for now, you have to get stronger and work hard in physical therapy."

My appearance told me how close to death I had been and could still be. I searched my reflection for signs of the strength and resolve of the woman I'd been, to somehow come to terms with the emaciated body and damaged face in the mirror. I had a choice. I could succumb to despair and be miserable, or I could gather every ounce of courage I could muster to accept my face and body, and to work like hell to get better. There was no point in living if I was going to be sad and unhappy. I chose life.

Later, I learned that for months, Mom had confided her opinion to friends and family that once I saw my scarred face and disfigured body, I wouldn't want to live. She was tormented that I might never forgive her for keeping me alive in this horrid condition. But on the other hand, Melissa fervently believed that I could survive anything, and despite my extensive injuries and the formidable challenges that I faced, I would want to live.

As the days and weeks passed, I felt like a mutant amid a planet of "normal-looking" people. It was hard to accept the incongruity of living with a deformity after being an attractive, desirable woman. People other than the hospital staff treated me differently because of my disfigurement. Strangers stared, gasped in shock, turned their eyes downward, or avoided me.

Moreover, smiling was impossible because the tight scar bands around my mouth prevented me from opening it normally. As a result, I was unable to show any realistic expression of my emotions for nearly a year.

Despite these significant obstacles, females tended to be receptive to me. There was a marked difference in the response of males. Before the accident, I had turned heads when men wanted to flirt with me; after, they bowed their heads in repulsion.

Yet I felt comfortable being with people who knew me before my injury. Family and longtime friends and associates seemed to understand my extensive losses and recognized my resilience. It upset me that strangers could not experience me as the woman trapped inside my altered body. Sometimes I would show photos of myself before the accident to new acquaintances, to help them understand who I really was. Unfortunately, most of them could not relate to the person in the photograph. They sensed the cruel loss but did not seem to connect to the "original" me.

CHAPTER EIGHT

A Glimpse of the Possibilities

A glimpse is not a vision. But to a man on a mountain road by night, a glimpse of the next three feet of road may matter more than a vision of the horizon.

C. S. Lewis

Four months after the crash

I had survived almost a month at the rehab hospital. It was a Friday afternoon in July, and Melissa was sitting across the room from me, sorting our mail. As I gazed out the window, I saw an iridescent hummingbird fluttering over a pink hibiscus bloom. It was always a gift to catch a glimpse of these magical little birds. I remembered my bike rides on Cat Island and how I'd enjoyed the crisp chirps of finches and the vibrant, tropical flowers. I relished the weekends and getting together with friends for dinner, playing tennis, swimming, shopping, or doing something else fun. Other than watching *Ellen*, *Home*

Improvement, and *Seinfeld* on TV, Melissa provided the only source of "fun" in my antiseptic environment.

Confined to my hospital bed, I couldn't sit up by myself or perform any normal everyday activities like brushing my teeth, eating, reading, or attending to my personal hygiene. I was disheartened that I couldn't do anything on my own and longed for my independence. All my caregivers reassured me with the same phrase: "In time, you'll regain strength and muscle tone; in time, you'll be able to perform ADLs" (activities of daily living). Every time someone said those words, I cringed.

The problem was, I wasn't convinced.

"I want to meet another burn survivor face to face," I told Melissa. "Someone who's doing well. I want to ask them how they feel now and how long it took them to return to their life." We had never known or seen anyone who had been burned, except for Kevin McGann; he had been severely burned in an automobile accident about eight weeks prior to my injury. He'd been sitting in his Mazda RX-7 at a stop sign when someone plowed into him from behind. The car burst into flames, and the driver's-side door was jammed shut. A brave bystander rushed over to the car, broke the window, and pulled Kevin out of the car.

But Kevin, like me, was also in the early stages of his recovery. I wanted to see the possibilities. Instead, I was living the limitations.

"Why don't we call the Phoenix Society?" Melissa said. "Rolando told me they might be able to help us and that the founder, Alan Breslau, also survived an airplane crash and extensive burns like yours. He said that Alan's face was almost destroyed." Rolando was a kind social worker at Jackson Memorial Hospital.

"Have you got the number?"

"I think I wrote it in my address book. Let's see . . . here. I have it." She read the number.

Thirty-one years earlier, severely burned victims like Alan rarely survived, so we knew that few people had lived through an airplane crash and an extensive burn injury. Surely, Alan and I would have much in common.

At the least, he might offer some comfort, but he might also provide practical ideas to help that hadn't occurred to me. In any event, we were kindred spirits on some level as crash and burn survivors. I anticipated that an encounter with him would be like two people desperately lost in the wilderness who suddenly see each other.

As Melissa dialed his number, I wondered if I would get to talk with Alan. I felt warm and excited. But it was close to 5:00 p.m., and I feared that the office might already be closed. My heart beat faster as she placed the receiver next to my melted ear.

At last, I will talk with someone who knows exactly what I'm going through, someone who has recovered and resumed a meaningful life. The ringing stopped, and a man answered: "The Phoenix Society, this is Alan. How can I help you?"

His voice was warm and approachable, just as I'd hoped.

"Hi, this is Charlene Pell. I'm a burn survivor. Do you have a few minutes to talk with me?"

"Sure. When and how were you burned?"

"Four months ago, sixty-four percent of my body was burned in a private-airplane crash in the Bahamas. As a result, my hands and face are severely disfigured."

"Was anyone else injured in the crash?"

My throat tightened as I replied, "Yes. My fiancé. The pilot. He died of sepsis twenty-one days after the crash."

"I'm so sorry, dear. You've been through a lot. How are you doing?"

"I'm happy to be alive but exasperated that I can't do anything by myself. My sister is holding the phone to what's left of my ear right now. It's humiliating and embarrassing. How long did it take for you to be able to return to your life?"

"It doesn't happen overnight, but, slowly, you'll regain your independence. So, try to view this period as a temporary state."

Temporary—I hadn't considered this idea before. This was just a phase of the recovery process that I must pass through to reach some sort of normalcy. This stage would reach an end, and I would improve.

I had become a slave to the monotonous routine of dressing changes, painful procedures, and therapies and felt like I was plodding along. I wanted to sprint to my former lifestyle.

Like me, he knew we were meeting on a rare plane of existence, and as we spoke, we established an immediate rapport.

"Where are you being treated?"

"Initially, I was at Jackson Memorial Hospital in Miami. Then, three weeks ago, I was transferred to HealthSouth Rehabilitation Hospital in Sunrise, Florida."

"Do you have family there with you?"

"Yes, my mother and sister have been by my side since I was hospitalized. They tried to transfer me to a rehabilitation hospital close to them in North Carolina. My insurer refused to pay for out-of-state care. This makes things really difficult for them."

"I'm not surprised about the insurer. Unfortunately, this happens to many people injured while traveling or out of town. You're very fortunate that your family has been able to arrange to be with you. How do you feel about the care you're receiving?"

"I felt safer at the Burn Center at Jackson Memorial. Here, the nurses have less experience treating burn survivors. They're kind and accommodating, but sometimes I feel like I'm instructing them through the dressing changes. They're cautious during all the procedures. It takes most of the nurses twice as long to complete the dressing changes. Afterward, I feel exhausted and agitated."

"The nurses at the burn units are highly specialized. It's hard to find the same expertise in rehabilitation hospitals. You said that your face and hands were badly burned. Have you accepted your changed appearance?"

It took me a moment to respond in a measured voice.

"I wish my face had been spared, but it wasn't, so I'll just have to adjust to it. Right now, I'm more concerned about regaining my strength and independence."

"One thing I've learned, Charlene . . . may I call you that?"

"Of course."

"One thing I've learned is that what's past is over. You need to concentrate on the future, which means seeing who you are now and learning to accept it. You must let go of your former appearance and make the best of your new self. When I created the Phoenix Society, I chose the name because, as burn survivors, we must arise from the fire and flames, like the legendary phoenix, and become more beautiful than before. Do you think that you can do that?"

"More beautiful than before." *That sounds lovely, but how can it be true?* "Oddly," I said, "I think I'm coming to terms with my disfigurement. I'm both comforted and tortured looking at photos of myself from before the crash. I know that I'll never look or be the same. Nothing about my burned face resembles my former appearance at all, except for my eyes."

Everyone I had met since the accident told me that my hazel eyes were beautiful. Most likely, people had to focus on my eyes to connect with me as a human being. Even though my right eyelid was contracted and my eyebrows had been seared, my eyes were the most visible part of my body that didn't look abnormal.

Alan took a breath as if he wanted to tell me something important. "I don't think of myself as being disfigured. I think

I look great when I put on my hairpiece in the morning. My ear is plastic, but you can't really tell. My whole face is reconstructed, but I've always had a good self-image, so it doesn't bother me. It took a while, of course, but I can now do just about everything I used to do. I play tennis every week and drive on my own wherever I need to go. You learn how to adapt to the changes in your body. Wait and see—you'll be doing things you love. It just takes time, work, and determination."

Oh, there was that "time" word again. But it came from someone who knew firsthand precisely how much time and determination it takes to recover. Alan had been where I was at that moment, and in time, he'd gotten to where he was. He provided a realistic goal and the possibility of a mentor.

I appreciated his encouragement, but more importantly, he had shown me that it was possible to resume my life again. Truly possible! I didn't know if he had lost someone as I had, but he seemed to have found a way to surmount the many obstacles along this road. Melissa was tiring—she switched the phone to her other hand—but she looked eager to hear what Alan had said.

"You need to get involved in our organization. Other survivors will help you. You'll see how they've recovered and renewed their lives. I'll ask Ruth, our assistant, to send you a membership packet, and you can read all about the organization. You'll find that there are some survivors in Florida. Give them a call and introduce yourself. You need to attend the World Burn Congress."

I asked, "What's the World Burn Congress?"

"It's a gathering of burn survivors and health care professionals who meet annually to network and attend lectures and workshops about issues important to burn survivors. Several hundred burn survivors will attend."

"Really," I uttered in amazement.

"There are thousands of burn survivors. We just haven't been able to reach all of them yet."

That was a lot more than I had realized. The idea of meeting and interacting with other burn survivors appealed to me, especially if they'd found ways to live meaningful lives. Alan also told me about the American Burn Association (ABA) and its annual conference. He and his wife, Delwyn, attended every year.

"If you're able, why don't you plan to come to an ABA conference? We'll introduce you to other survivors, and you can attend workshops and programs about burns and rehabilitation."

I felt hopeful, like it was a special invitation for me. I would have to get stronger, and I prayed the goal would be achievable.

"I hope I'll be strong enough to attend. I'd love to meet you and Delwyn in person and learn more about the Phoenix Society. You've given me hope today. I can't thank you enough."

"You're going to be fine, dear. I can tell by the tone and intent in your voice. So, hang in there. Things will improve."

"Alan, thank you so much for the encouragement and information. I so look forward to meeting you face to face. Good night."

My voice was strained from the conversation, but I felt motivated and smiled at Melissa as the call came to an end.

Melissa removed the phone from my ear. She looked as if she'd been holding her breath. I smiled, barely aware of the pain from my dressing change. It was as if hope had flooded my body with a buffer, at least for that moment. I felt a tear roll down my cheek. As I looked at Melissa, I could tell she knew: I could see a future for the first time. I could reclaim my life.

A gauntlet of demanding physical therapy lined the road to the ABA conference, but I couldn't think about that. Nothing was going to stop me from getting to that group of survivors, to Alan, and to my new life.

And I was ready to fight for the right to do so.

CHAPTER NINE

Stepping Stones

It always seems impossible until it's done.

Nelson Mandela

First summer after the crash

Every weekday morning, someone transported me in a wheelchair to the hand clinic, where my occupational therapist, Sandi, removed the yellow-stained dressings from my hands and cleaned my open wounds. My swollen, deformed, and blistered hands had fingers locked into a position similar to the crooked talons of an eagle. As Sandi extended and flexed my fingers, I grimaced in pain. But the result would be worth it: once I could touch my index finger to my thumb, I'd be able to pick up and hold objects.

Unfortunately, I probably would never be able to wear rings again. I hadn't thought about my engagement ring or tennis bracelet until I saw my misshapen fingers. Melissa told me that my ring had had to be cut off my finger in the operating room. She had it in safekeeping, but my diamond tennis bracelet was missing. It hadn't been found with the clothes I had left in my car before boarding the plane to Cat Island. The missing bracelet was the least of my concerns, given the monumental hurdles ahead. Regaining the use of my fingers and hands was all that mattered.

"Come on, push as hard as you can now," Sandi urged. "Try to make a fist."

There was a certain kind of buoyancy about Sandi as she briskly walked from one side of the room to the other. Usually, a white lab coat embroidered with her name covered her preppy clothes. She could have been a model for dental products with her bright-white smile and perfectly shaped, upturned nose. She was skilled and demanding yet compassionate.

To distract me from the pain, she said, "I thought about you during the weekend while biking. Didn't you say that you used to go for bike rides on Cat Island?"

Happy to talk about it, I said, "Almost every Saturday I spent there, I went for a fifteen- to twenty-mile ride. It was always an adventure and fun." First, I'd pass by the iron gate covered with royal-blue morning glories that separated our property from Hawk's Nest. Then I'd ride down the gravel road to the two-lane road that encircled the island.

"It was unnerving when I had to pass through Hawk's Nest, a clothing-optional resort adjacent to our property! The only access to the main road was through this resort. So I rode through as fast as possible, hoping I wouldn't catch a glimpse of any of the guests who walked about naked, nonchalantly unaffected by my presence."

Sandi blushed as she said, "Oh my, that must have been awkward!"

"I never got used to it. I'd pedal as fast as I could until I was hidden by palm trees. Then I'd slow to the rhythm of their fronds bending in the ocean breeze. The tropical landscape was dotted with square cinder-block huts with blue doors to ward off evil spirits. Some islanders were very superstitious. Such beliefs still exist in the States; in the South, some people still believe that a darker blue, a 'haint blue,' keeps evil spirits away. The beliefs are passed down from generation to generation."

"Oh wow, that's amazing," Sandi said.

"I'd stop alongside the road and visit the straw lady, often purchasing a handwoven basket of some sort. Ouch!"

Sandi backed off a little but then pushed on my finger again. "Go on. The straw lady," she prompted.

I took a steadying breath and sank back into thoughts of my island paradise. "It was always challenging to balance a large basket while maneuvering the bike." I looked at my hands, wondering if I'd ever be able to grasp handlebars again. "Sometimes I grabbed an ice-cold beer for the trip back to the Rock. I didn't usually like beer, but on a long bike ride, there was nothing more refreshing. By the time I returned to our house at Dolphin Head Point, I was invigorated and ready to cool off with a swim."

"Your rides sound much more intriguing than mine." Sandi sensed my unspoken question. "Someday, you'll be able to ride a bike again."

It was uplifting to be with Sandi. As the months passed, we became friends. I lived vicariously through her. Like me, she loved biking, skiing, tennis, and swimming. Once, when she was recounting a recent ski trip, I fondly recalled my ski escapades with Roger in Colorado. I longed to be there with him. I cried, knowing that skiing and Roger existed only in my past. I yearned for my former lifestyle, which had become nothing more than steam disappearing into the atmosphere.

One thing I enjoyed about the hand clinic was that various patients were treated simultaneously. One day in July, I met an adorable eleven-year-old boy with dark-brown hair and long black eyelashes—and several missing fingers due to a fireworks accident on the Fourth of July. He appeared to be coping with his loss better than his mom was. He was being treated as an outpatient. I watched longingly as he left the clinic casually, swinging his arms and walking with ease. Unable to walk independently, I still had to rely on others to take me to therapy in the wheelchair. I couldn't maneuver the wheelchair alone because of my severely injured hands. And meeting the little boy's mom reminded me of the days when I, too, could dress in stylish clothes, wear heels, and feel like an attractive woman. I had become the antithesis of everything that I once had been. Being with these people only reminded me that I would never again be considered normal. But I was lucky. Sandi and her associate, Linda, never made me feel inferior or less than anyone. Instead, they empowered me to work diligently to regain my life and dreams. Often, they reminded me, "This is hard, painful work, but you have to do it to get better."

Hard work was nothing new for me. Throughout my life, I have been a hard worker and have strived to be the best at whatever I did. In school, I studied to make the honor roll and practiced to excel in sports like acrobatics and gymnastics. I wasn't the most intelligent person in the class or the best in sports, but often I was the most determined, committed, and passionate about my goals. In junior and senior high school, I longed to be a cheerleader. In the backyard, I practiced routines, cartwheels, handstands, and walkovers months before tryouts. Year after year, I was the "runner-up." Heartbroken and devastated, I would retreat to my bedroom, light a candle, and cry while listening to soothing New Age music. After a couple of hours, I'd emerge with tear-stained cheeks but determined to try out again the following year. Finally, my perseverance paid off when I was elected school mascot.

As had been necessary back then, I had to channel my determination and perseverance into the hardest challenge of my life: regaining my strength, stamina, function, and mobility and, most importantly, my independence.

After the hand clinic, Mom or Melissa would take me back to my room and feed me lunch. I couldn't eat unassisted because my right elbow was locked at a thirty-degree angle. A condition called heterotrophic ossification caused lack of motion in the joint. Even with the aid of an adaptive device attached to my wrist with Velcro, I couldn't lift the modified spoon to my mouth. Melissa pureed most of my food in a processor, to fit through the tiny opening between my contracted lips. To my embarrassment, much of my meal dripped onto the bib that I didn't want to wear. This was especially humiliating.

I hated to be fed by others. I never imagined how the same process could be so different, depending on who was feeding me. My mom's companion, Hal, was my favorite. Hal painstakingly placed a tiny amount of food on the spoon so that I could consume it in one bite. Hal's handling of me reminded me of a sculptor, meticulously chiseling a piece of marble into a masterpiece. Every little morsel mattered to him. Hal was the gold standard, and no one else could ever please me as well as he did. That made me more determined than ever to find a way to eat unaided.

After a few weeks had passed, I asked my mom, "Doesn't this hospital have a cafeteria? I want to eat with other people. If they can't cope with my appearance, that's their problem. This is who I am, and I'm doing the best I can."

My mom looked surprised and happy. "Sure. Would you like to go today?"

I did. I was tired of my isolation. So Mom pushed my wheelchair to the cafeteria. Entering the room was like stepping into Penn Station in Manhattan for the first time. My eyes panned back and forth across the room as unfamiliar sounds drew my attention: The clock ticking. The trays being picked up. The loud conversations. The hushed whispers. Quickly, I tried to process the information overload and decide what to do next. Everywhere I looked, people were busy, talking and laughing. Hospital workers, patients, and visitors stood in line to order a hot meal or sandwich. Most of the hospital workers congregated at rectangular tables near the windows in the back of the room. Outside, I could see some picnic tables and a patio. There were people in wheelchairs and on crutches; others used walkers to get about. Notes were posted on bulletin boards about upcoming special events.

"Mom," I said, "let's go to the salad and sandwich bar, and I'll select what I want." The pungent aromas of tuna fish and ripe melons filled the air. Mom maneuvered my wheelchair close to a table and retrieved a tray. Looking around, I didn't notice anyone else with burns. Still, I found comfort in seeing plenty of other patients in the cafe.

This was the first step I took to be with "normal" people in a safe and nonthreatening environment. Despite my limitations, I felt like I fit in with the other patients. However, at times, I felt self-conscious when I sensed others staring.

My respite didn't last long. Rehab grew more demanding. I had to comply with a multitude of treatments and procedures simultaneously. Several times my physical therapist, a slender, ballerina-like lady named Margaret, cast my ankle and instructed me to do leg lifts from sitting and lying positions three times a day. The goal of the casting was to help me regain joint flexibility and normal range of motion in my ankle. At the same time, Sandi made a new splint for my right hand and told me to wear it for at least three hours a day. My humorous occupational therapist outside of the hand clinic, Adrienne, inserted and clasped an orthodontic-like metal and plastic device, called a microstomia-prevention apparatus, horizontally inside my mouth and locked it in place. Like a shoehorn, it stretched the contracted scar bands around my mouth for three hours daily, to maintain the opening. With this device in place, I couldn't eat, drink, or talk. Although I had become adept at juggling multiple projects simultaneously through my work experience, the concurrent treatments, medical devices, and procedures sometimes overwhelmed me, creating additional stress and pressure.

At the same time, I had to wear pressure garments on my entire body twenty-three hours a day, to minimize scarring and increase circulation to promote healing. I cried the day I was first fitted for the pressure garments. Designed to be "skintight," like a wet suit for diving, the custom-made garments were restrictive and hot. They made me feel like my frail and wounded body was being squeezed into a spandex outfit at least five sizes too small. As Sandi and Linda pressed my arms into the sleeves, I cried out, "This is insane to force my arms into this thing. Can't you see that this is breaking down my skin?" After working so diligently, I felt nauseous to see my skin tear from the pulling and tugging required to squish my trunk and arms into the pressure garments.

I thought there must be a way to design a garment that would not cause so much damage to my delicate skin. So I asked Sandi, "Couldn't the sleeves be closed with Velcro, instead of seamed together?"

"That would probably decrease the effectiveness of the garment," she said, "but I'll ask the manufacturer."

I was satisfied when a new garment arrived, made with Velcro closures. Because Sandi and Linda were receptive to my input, we found a practical solution that was less painful and harmful to my skin. It was rewarding to advocate for and receive what I believed I needed.

The day that Mom and Hal came to say goodbye before they left to return to Greensboro, Melissa and I met them at the nurses' station. I was sitting in a wheelchair, wearing a purple blouse and culottes. A five-by-three-inch piece of yellow Xeroform dressing was stuck across my forehead. My arms were wrapped in Tubigrip, a stretchy, ribbed, Band-Aid–colored pressurized fabric. Mom's face was already stained with tears as she prepared to say goodbye. "This is awful," she said. "I'm excited about returning to Greensboro, but I don't want to leave you, girls." "We don't want you to leave but realize that you need to." I was harboring a secret goal, and it was time to deliver. "It's okay. We'll be fine."

As Mom leaned closer, I placed my bandaged hands on the chair's armrests and slowly lifted myself into a standing position. Tears spilled onto Mom's cheeks as I reached out to gently hug her. Hal's smile beamed. "Look at you. By the time we return, we won't be able to keep up with you!" Melissa snapped a photo to commemorate a milestone that felt no less significant than the liftoff of the space shuttle. On that same day, I held a toothbrush for the first time and walked twenty-five feet with a walker, with Melissa by my side. It was an exhilarating day of new achievements.

Like a tightrope walker, I had to consciously think about the placement of each foot, to maintain my balance. Something I once had taken for granted became monumental. When I became sturdier, I got wheels on my walker. From there, I began to walk with the assistance of a three-pronged cane, and then, one glorious day, I walked on my own, unassisted. It was divine to travel about the hospital, holding on to the hallway handrails—to go and come as I pleased. Each new accomplishment motivated me to work harder to regain strength and mobility.

Once I could transfer from a wheelchair to inside a car, I could leave the hospital for several hours on a pass with a family member. It had been six months since I had ridden in a car. For days, my occupational therapists worked with Melissa and me so that we could execute the transfer. On our first thrill ride, in sunlight so bright I had to squint, we cruised around the rehab hospital parking lot. Moving at only fifteen miles an hour, I pushed my feet against the floor as if to put on the brakes. I felt like we were traveling sixty or seventy miles per hour! This must have been some sort of perceptual aberration.

Melissa and I were so excited to obtain our first pass. She took me to the apartment where she was temporarily staying. There, I sat on a genuine sofa for the first time since the accident. We snacked on some of my favorite appetizers—seeded crackers with smoked-whitefish dip from the Ocean Harvest market and goat cheese, sun-dried tomato, and basil spread— and watched the Miami Dolphins play football. It was such a memorable day. "I feel like a real person again," I told Melissa. It was renewing to be in a different environment outside of the hospital; however, being in an unfamiliar apartment also felt awkward and rekindled my desire to return to the cozy condo where Roger and I had lived. Still, I knew that was impossible because Roger's children had forced Mom and Melissa to remove my furniture and belongings from the condo while I was in a coma. All my possessions were in storage. Despite all the undesirable changes, I loved being with Melissa away from the hospital. We had such a good time that we barely made it back to the rehab hospital before curfew.

Melissa and me on our first pass to leave the hospital

Before, Saturdays and Sundays were depressing at the hospital because my therapists were all off, and part-time staff worked. Time seemed to drag by because I rarely had any therapy.

On our initial overnight pass, Melissa took me to the movies. This was a first for me—out in public with other people. She retrieved my wheelchair from the trunk and transferred me into it from the car. She then pushed me into the theater and locked the wheels into place near the back row. While I wanted to feel happy, I was sure the wheelchair would come loose, roll down the aisle, and crash into the screen. My sense of sight and sound were incredibly heightened, and I was aware of people staring at me. My horribly burned complexion made me look like a creature they'd never seen. Nevertheless, I tried to refocus my concentration on the movie. That was the point of being there, after all.

The film, *Forrest Gump*, was fabulous and heartwarming. Everything was going along fine, but in one scene, there was a fiery explosion.

"Oh my God," Melissa said, "I didn't know that there were explosions in this film!" We looked at one another in disbelief. I knew she thought she'd been instrumental in bringing back memories of that tragic day that had changed my life. But fortunately, the rest of the movie was just fine, and I relaxed. Cautiously, I even ate some popcorn, trying not to let the panic that I might choke stop me. I knew that if I was ever going to have even the semblance of an everyday life, I had to get past the fear that threatened each moment of my existence.

At the theater, I also tried to use a standard toilet. I didn't remember toilets being so low to the ground. As I went to sit down, I felt like I would never reach the seat. And then, once down, another thought nearly paralyzed me: What if I didn't have the strength to lift myself upright again? Amazingly, I managed to push myself up and get back into the wheelchair.

I was exhausted from the outing but encouraged and happy to do something that I used to do and love before my injury.

A few days later, Marvin Danto, founder of DCOTA, and Joan, my boss and the executive vice president, visited me. "Dear, here's some eggplant parmesan from one of your favorite restaurants, according to Vikki," Joan said as she handed two bags to Melissa. Vikki had been my go-to colleague at DCOTA.

"How's our girl doing today?" Marvin said.

"Better because you're here. Thank you so much for coming, Mr. D. I know how busy you are."

Marvin reached into the inside pocket of his tailored jacket. He pulled out a rectangular package wrapped in gold foil with a white taffeta bow. "Here is something I promised to get for you while you were in intensive care."

Melissa held the box close to me as she opened it. I was shocked to see a stunning gold diamond tennis bracelet inside! "Oh, Mr. D., it's exquisite. Would you please put it on my wrist?"

"Of course, I'd love to."

Melissa handed the bracelet to Mr. D., and he carefully clasped it over the Tubigrip dressing on my arm. It was the only piece of jewelry that I had worn since my injury. Wearing the bracelet and seeing it glimmer in the light made me feel feminine for the first time since the crash.

"I'll always treasure this moment and your love and devotion," I said as I fought back the tears.

I now recalled that he'd promised to buy me a diamond bracelet to replace the missing one that Roger had given to me. Still, I had dismissed this as a gracious sentiment and never dreamed he would actually do it.

My thoughts flashed back to the day of the accident when I had reached for my bracelet and had the eerie premonition. I wondered what had happened to my diamond tennis bracelet.

CHAPTER TEN

Compassionate Caregivers

Can we create a place of healing that helps her
transcend beyond her physical limitations?

Bonnie Wesorick

Five months after the crash

A tall, solid fellow with dimples and curly black hair appeared in the doorway of my room while I was sitting in my wheelchair and reading a card from a friend.

"Hi, my name is Howard. I'm a massage therapist. Dr. Sassoon says you've been suffering from tight muscles in your neck and shoulders and that you asked about massage. Do you feel like giving it a try?"

I paused for a minute, remembering how painful it was for anyone to touch me; I was desperate for some relief but skeptical. Since my hospitalization, anyone who'd touched me was intent on drawing blood, checking blood pressure, tending a wound, performing painful stretches, or preparing me for another surgical procedure.

"I'd like to try it, but there's only a small patch of skin on the back of my neck that isn't burned. I don't think that I can tolerate touch anywhere else."

"I'll be gentle. Just let me know if you want me to stop."

Howard walked behind me and placed his warm, firm fingers on my neck's tiny, only patch of normal skin. He applied light pressure.

"Does this feel okay?"

"Yes, it feels good." This was the first time that anyone had applied a comforting touch in more than five months. "Most people hesitate to touch me, worried they might hurt me. I appreciate their concern. Nevertheless, I do miss being touched. I'm fragile, but a gentle pat or hug would be good."

"Touch is an important aspect of life and healing."

I began to relax while Howard massaged my neck and asked, "What kind of art do you like?"

"I paint in my spare time."

"What do you typically paint?" My neck felt warm and tingly as blood rushed through the tissue.

"Cityscapes or landscapes, usually. There's going to be an exhibit of my paintings in my hometown in New Jersey in a few months."

"That's fabulous." For a minute, I imagined myself getting out to see an art exhibit. I'd always loved visiting art galleries and boutiques.

"I have several paintings in our office. You can see them there after you're discharged."

"I can't wait to see your paintings and to be able to visit your office for treatments. To have a normal life. Finally."

"I'm sure you do. You've been through quite a lot." His voice softened. "So, would you like me to return next week? Thursday, about this same time?"

"Sounds great, thank you."

Howard just about filled the doorframe as he left my room.

It was ironic that such a tall, gentle giant of a man could be so tender and compassionate. From that day, Howard continued to return to give me a brief, gentle massage on any skin he could find that could tolerate touch.

The rehab hospital had never allowed a massage therapist into the facility until Dr. Sassoon arranged for Howard to treat me at my request. Dr. Sassoon directed my rehabilitation team like an accomplished conductor of a symphony. He listened to my concerns, fears, and difficulties. Sympathetic and attentive, he was open to my ideas and suggestions.

Like any other burn patient, I was in a fight to save my life and regain my independence.

Nearly every weekday afternoon at about 3:00 p.m., Dr. Mic, my psychologist, appeared at the entrance to my room with a wheelchair to whisk me away to his office. There, we talked about whatever was on my mind that day. Most afternoons, I was tired and agitated from physical and occupational therapy and, frankly, from eating lunch. Every movement and activity drained my limited energy. After lying in a hospital bed for more than three months, my muscles had atrophied. I had lost twenty-five pounds and barely weighed one hundred. However, I was always eager to see Dr. Mic appear at my door.

As he pushed my wheelchair through the wide, bright hallway to his office, we sometimes passed a young woman in a bathrobe walking with an aide, nurses and visitors, or a technician pushing the mobile X-ray machine. During weekdays, the rehab hospital bustled with activity; over the weekends, it was quiet, like a tent after the circus leaves.

When Dr. Mic first introduced himself, he looked more like a graduate student than an experienced psychologist. He was a fit, blond, handsome guy with an Ivy League look, who I imagined couldn't have a clue about what it must feel like to be disfigured. I wondered if he could understand what I'd been through and how on earth someone so young and unexperienced could help me, but I decided to give him a chance. His broad smile was welcoming and friendly, and his blue eyes reminded me of the mesmerizing eyes of a Weimaraner dog. He was married and had a toddler. His first words surprised me.

"It looks like many people miss and need you from all the cards and gifts I see."

I relaxed. Perhaps he had read the article about me and the accident in the *Sun Sentinel* newspaper, describing my executive role at DCOTA. He understood. He knew what I needed. I smiled, and that small gesture connected us. I was ready to put myself into his care.

Psychology fascinated me, as it had been my major in college. Early in my career, I worked as a psychiatric social worker at Broughton Hospital. So it was comforting to be familiar with at least one aspect of my rehabilitation.

His office was hardly an oasis of calm, even when it was just the two of us. Three tall stacks of what I imagined were charts and professional papers teetered on his desk, with more on the shelves and floor. It felt stressful to me, as if he had a large backlog of work to do. Pastel watercolors of sailboats and other scenes from Greece, live hanging plants, and soothing jazz playing in the background countered my first impression. He may have been busy, but he knew how to surround himself with reminders to relax. The office felt cozy, not institutional, with its subdued lighting. Hundreds of books about assisting people through crisis and trauma lined the bookshelves.

During my sessions with Dr. Mic, I told him about things that I couldn't always share with Mom and Melissa. In a sense, Mom and Melissa had lost the daughter and sister they had loved and had often turned to for assistance and direction. I realized their suffering and loss, and I didn't want to add to their anguish and stress. They were coping with their own challenges. I didn't want to overburden them.

The dynamics of our family had shifted in the way that the unsecured contents of a car slide when you slam on the brakes to avert a crash. In our prior lives, Mom and Melissa had relied on me in times of crisis and counted on my input on important issues. Mom often told people about how my intervention had possibly saved my stepfather's life. He had been gravely ill, and I had insisted that he be transferred to a more qualified hospital equipped to treat his condition. He recovered from a severe pulmonary illness and lived for several more years.

Melissa had nearly died in an auto accident in 1986. She was in a coma for more than a week. At the time, I was working in Memphis. I immediately flew to Wilmington, North Carolina, to help Mom and to oversee Melissa's care. Months later, Melissa moved to Memphis to live with me while she continued her recuperation.

Now, our roles had reversed. In my state after the crash, I was more like an infant than a competent, mature adult, and they had been thrown into the role of caregivers. Uprooted from their own lives. Melissa had quit her beloved job at an art gallery in Wilmington; Mom was a funeral director who worked on commission and had lost a great deal of income from sales she'd been unable to make. At times, they must have been resentful and disappointed and wished their lives hadn't been interrupted. I sensed that they were constantly torn between wanting to be by my side and longing to be home with their companions. Despite their stoic attempts to hide their feelings, I could tell I was a burden.

The most upsetting incident occurred when the father of Melissa's boyfriend, Ryan, died on Valentine's Day in 1995. Ryan and his dad were very close, and Ryan was devastated by his father's sudden death from a heart attack. I knew that Melissa longed to be with Ryan, and I offered to travel with her to Wilmington. She was heartbroken when Ryan told her that he didn't want her to bring me. He said, "If you bring Charlene, all the attention will be on her, not Dad."

I, too, had met Ryan's dad and had been around him on many occasions. I told Melissa that I would stay at a hotel so that she could be with Ryan and attend the funeral. She felt terrible for me and decided not to go. She later regretted this tough decision.

I could confide in Dr. Mic about things like that. In one session, I told him about my fear of never experiencing love and intimacy. For a fleeting moment, I recalled feeling and looking sexy and pretty in my lavender satin nighty. "There will never be a man I'm interested in who will ever be able to get beyond my appearance to love me. It's sad to know that I'll never experience the excitement of a kiss, the arousal of touch, the passion of making love. Oh, sure, I'll have male friends, but that's not the same."

He responded, "Many people with physical challenges have intimate relationships and find love. As you become more comfortable with your altered appearance, your feelings may change."

I felt most at ease with people who knew me before I was burned. They could appreciate the staggering losses I had experienced, physically, emotionally, and professionally. Strangers who met me realized that, obviously, something catastrophic had happened to me, but they couldn't grasp the depth of my losses, suffering, or sorrow. How could they understand unless they had personally experienced something similar?

"Sometimes people act like I have a disease. I'm tempted to wear a T-shirt that reads 'I survived a burn injury: it's not contagious!'"

It really annoyed me when strangers approached and asked Melissa questions about me. Melissa fired back the response, "Why don't you ask her? She's right here."

I needed Dr. Mic, to off-load my frustration and achieve a more useful frame of mind.

"Isn't it enough I have to deal with rehab, surgery, dressing changes, limited mobility, and physical challenges without educating the public about burn injuries?"

"Try to stay in the present and not worry about the future," Dr. Mic said. "Take one day at a time. You're making great progress. I know you want to accelerate the process, but it takes time."

"Seems like everyone is telling me that, and I'm sick of it. Time! It's all I'm looking at. Will I ever have a normal life again?"

Dr. Mic reassured me that my life would be different than before but that I could be happy and fulfilled again. He felt confident that I would be able to return to work at DCOTA "in time."

"The woman who's doing my job is the person I mentored. I didn't intend for her to take my job! This is so upsetting after all that I did to earn that position. It's been taken from me through no fault of my own."

"Someone has to step in during your absence to keep the company afloat. I understand that your boss and the owner have visited several times and that they continue to seek your opinion about projects."

I appreciated that Mr. D. and Joan valued my opinion, but I was sad that I couldn't be at DCOTA working. I longed for the day that I could return.

More than anything, I wanted to regain my independence, so I worked one day at a time to set attainable goals to reclaim my self-sufficiency. As part of that process, I focused on the day I would once again live on my own and return to work at DCOTA. Dr. Mic then began to ask, "What is your plan to move you closer to the goal of returning to work?"

He helped me to concentrate on precisely what I needed to

do as I took small steps to regain my independence and my former life during the following days, weeks, and months. I read reports and trade magazines to stay informed about the design industry, events, and projects and strived to gain strength and increase mobility.

Four o'clock ended our sessions and returned me to my room to prepare for my least favorite time of the day, shower time. I dreaded going to the shower room; it was sheer torture. Day after day, I had to swallow two Darvocet painkillers twenty minutes before the shower just to get through it. My primary nurse, Marilyn, would undress me and transfer me from my wheelchair to a shower chair, a contraption that looked like it had been constructed from white PVC plumbing tubes. There was a hole in the center of the chair, similar to that in a toilet seat. Marilyn covered me with a sheet and whisked me in the chair across the hallway to the shower room. She had the unpleasant task of meticulously picking black scabs off my scalp while the tepid water beat down on my raw skin. As the water swept away the scabs, they looked like roaches skittering into the drain. Often the sores became infected and oozed with a lemonade-yellow puss. Most days, I cried throughout the ordeal. My skin was so inflamed that the lightest spray from the water caused searing pain. I wanted to be clean and fresh, but the process was agonizing.

There were five stalls with ivory fabric curtains for privacy. Marilyn discreetly bathed me, attentive to my privacy, which I appreciated. Before my injury, I had always been modest. Since the crash, so many strangers had seen my naked body that I was becoming accustomed to the intrusion. Someday, I would be able to shower in the one in my room.

"In time."

Following the shower, Marilyn applied medication to my tender scalp and sterile dressings to my wounds. By the time she completed the tedious process, I felt drained.

Often, I endured the agonizing experience of feeling as if snails were creeping across my face, and the space between my nose and lips felt like a wet sponge. It was nearly unbearable and unaffected by medication. Desperately, I searched for distractions to refocus my attention. Watching television helped sometimes. I prayed for strength to get through the miserable, bizarre sensations.

During my counseling sessions with Dr. Mic, I spoke of my love for jazz, New Age, and classical music. From these discussions, he sensed that the melodies would comfort me. One Monday evening, on his way home, he stopped by my room to give me music tapes he had recorded over the weekend. "I think you'll like these. They're some of my favorites!"

This gracious act reinforced Dr. Mic's genuine concern for me. He was fully invested in my successful recovery.

I felt like I had lost everything that truly mattered to me, except for Mom, Melissa, some of my friends, my renewed faith, and my mind. Confined to room 105, unable to care for myself, I quickly learned how unimportant material things were to life. I realized I could survive as long as I had my family, faith, and hope. I would find a way to go on in the face of so much heartbreaking loss and disappointment.

That night, as I lay in bed with the lights turned out except for the soft glow of the ginger jar lamp on the dresser across from the bed, I listened to calming instrumentals by Earl Klugh, Boney James, and Windham Hill and became attached to them. I recalled how I loved to listen to this kind of music as I drove home from work, with the wind blowing in my hair. The music transported me to memories of happy times. It was bittersweet. Throughout my stay at the rehab hospital, I listened to these tapes in the early hours of the evening and before I went to sleep. I focused my attention on the tranquil arrangements, and music became the one medication that truly soothed my seared spirit and body.

Like irreplaceable heirlooms, I treasured the cassette tapes that Dr. Mic took the time to record for me while I was a patient at HealthSouth Sunrise Rehabilitation Hospital. It's difficult to explain what a profound meaning this music had and continues to have in my life. Every time I hear recordings that were on the tapes, I fondly remember the kindness and insightful thoughtfulness of Dr. Mic. I am eternally indebted to him for his counseling and compassion and for teaching me how to find a way through formidable circumstances and challenges to regain my identity and my life.

Contrary to what the medical profession advocates, I believe that the best care providers are those who know how to connect with their patients. Those caregivers who develop meaningful relationships with their patients offer superior care and nurture healing.

Not all my caregivers were kind; some stole my clothes and medication while I sat in the shower. Some were incompetent and should not have been permitted to provide care. One nurse at the rehab hospital took hours to change my dressings and discussed her frustrations with the hospital the entire time. I felt like a hostage, unable to escape the mental stress. As a vulnerable patient unable to perform basic tasks independently, I didn't feel comfortable confronting the nurse about her behavior. I'd be at her mercy. Instead, I diverted the conversation whenever possible to more-pleasant topics. Once I was stronger, I requested another nurse for the dressing changes.

Overall, I was blessed to have primarily exceptional care providers who were highly skilled, dedicated, compassionate, and honest. I could detect when others were simply "doing their job."

Howard was one of the former. Once the skin-graft donor sites began to heal, his massages became more soothing. The donor sites were where healthy skin on my back had been surgically separated from the blood supply and transplanted to cover open wounds on my arms. Unfortunately, the pain from a donor site was excruciating for the first few days after the surgery.

But the endless stretches of pain-filled time were broken up by my highly anticipated sessions with Howard, one of my most caring providers.

CHAPTER ELEVEN

I'll Be Seeing You . . .

you're everywhere
except right here
and it hurts

Rupi Kaur

Eight months after the crash

After discharge from the rehab hospital, I moved back to Port Royale, into a different condo in the same building where Roger and I had shared so much love and so many happy memories. My grieving was intense. Everywhere I looked, I thought of him. Everywhere I went, I passed by places dear to us. It was agonizing to drive past Sage, a charming French restaurant we used to frequent—the spot where we'd eaten dinner the evening before the crash.

Much to the amazement of my burn doctors, I was driving. They had told Mom and Melissa that, most likely, I would never drive again. Regrettably, I had agreed to sell my fabulous convertible because of the doctors' inaccurate prediction. I could only imagine the shock and trepidation the state trooper who rode with me during my driving test must have felt when he first met me. I was bandaged from head to toe in pressure garments and wore a Uvex face mask, gloves, and a decorative red Christmas vest, skort, and black tennis shoes. Most likely, he had never seen anyone who looked like me. I was determined to pass the test and prove I could drive. And to my surprise and relief, the kind and compassionate state trooper was patient and supportive. He appeared to want me to succeed.

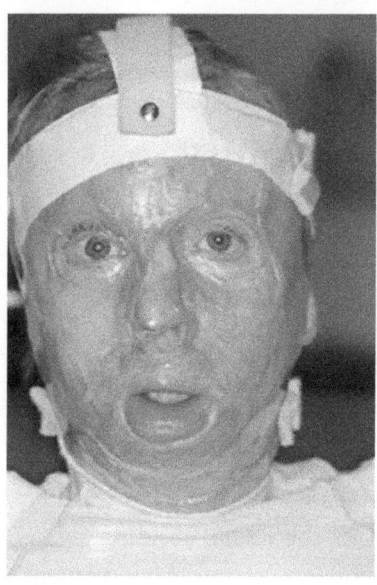

The Uvex mask

For months before the crash, I'd been learning to play the song "I'll Be Seeing You." I loved the lyrics and melody, although playing or hearing it always made me teary-eyed and overcome with emotion. I never imagined living the reality of the lyrics so soon. "Unforgettable" was another song that triggered a flood of tears as I recalled dancing to it with Roger in the candlelight of the kitchen at our home on Cat Island. "Misty" reminded me of nights in Beaver Creek, Colorado, when the song played while we listened in a cozy corner of one of our favorite restaurants. We loved to sit at the fireside table on cold winter evenings. Hearing the melodies we'd treasured conjured precious memories yet sometimes felt like a bee sting, with its unexpected, lingering pain.

I missed waking up to the aroma of fresh coffee brewing.

Every morning, Roger had brought coffee to me in one of the mugs we'd acquired on our various trips. My favorite mug was from Maine and featured an exquisite painting of a loon. Every August, Roger and I had traveled to Maine for his family's annual reunion. We stayed in a little cottage by a lake. Nightly, we built a bonfire and sat outside in the moonlight, listening to the spellbinding cries of the loons. I had never seen a loon, except in a movie, until I had met Roger. The loons were mesmerizing. They always seemed so far away—too far away to see the intricate details of their majestic plumage. One of the many exciting new experiences that Roger had brought into my life was spotting the loons and hearing their cries.

I wondered if I would ever again see a loon or be able to travel to Maine to see where Roger had been buried.

I understood how it felt to be blindsided by emotion sparked by ordinary experiences. I recalled a day out shopping with Mom. We were at a Hallmark store to buy some cards. I looked up from the rack of cards and saw Mom crying. I asked why.

"I'll never be able to buy another birthday card for my sister." Mom's sister had died about a year before the incident at Hallmark. Mom had outlived her six siblings.

I also remembered Mom telling me that, many years after his death, she'd never felt as alone in the world as she had the day my father, her husband, had died.

Twice after Roger's death, I had the unnerving experience of seeing a man who appeared to be just like him. The first time, I was walking to the elevator after parking in the garage at the condominium. Just before the elevator door closed, a man identical to Roger entered. He glanced at me, turned around, and exited the floor before mine, leaving me stunned and shaken. The second time was while driving. Again, I saw a man who looked exactly like Roger, wearing his trademark panama hat, in my rearview mirror. It was all I could do to stay

calm and focused enough to drive. Yet, weirdly, it was comforting. As if he was keeping an eye on me.

I had a similar experience after my dad died. One night,
when I was driving home from a graduate class at Appalachian
State University, I saw a man who seemed to be identical to
my father walking on the side of the road, in the middle of no-
where. Shocked and startled, I looked in the rearview mirror,
and he disappeared into the fog.

It has been confusing, yet reassuring, to see Dad and
Roger—or apparitions of them—after their deaths. No doubt
there will be people who do not believe me, but that's okay because I know what I saw. The memories are unforgettable. I
was not under the influence of any drug or alcohol when I had
these existential experiences. I will leave it up to thanatolo-
gists to determine what I saw.

On nights cool enough for me to venture outdoors and
onto the balcony overlooking the Intracoastal Waterway and
the ocean, the wind blowing across my face reminded me of
the night I met Roger. We walked under the stars, alongside
the shore. The only pauses in our conversation were filled with
the soothing sound of the wind and the undulating waves
crashing upon the shore, leaving a bubbly, momentary white
foam in their wake. I was wearing a long skirt, and the edges
got wet in the surf, as did the bottoms of Roger's slacks. We
lingered for an hour, and then Roger asked if I wanted to go to
his place. I said, "Yes."

CHAPTER TWELVE

Traveling Home for Christmas

Remembrance, like a candle, shines brightest at Christmastime.

Charles Dickens

Nine months after the crash

It was Christmastime, and Melissa and I were going home to Greensboro to spend the holidays with Mom. It was the first time I had flown since the accident. I was apprehensive about flying but eager to return home. I missed the colder weather. It never felt like Christmas in Florida because of the tropical climate and landscape. Days before the trip, we started preparing. We tried to pack our suitcases as efficiently as possible since I wouldn't be able to help with the luggage. An entire carry-on bag was filled with sterile gauze pads; Tubigrip; ointments; tape; pressure garments for my trunk, arms, and legs; splints for my hands and arms; and all the supplies that we would need to change bandages and care for open wounds.

We left for Fort Lauderdale International Airport early to

allow plenty of time to check our luggage and clear security. I was walking unassisted but had not been in large crowds of people rushing to make connections for flights. I was fragile, physically and emotionally. As we walked through the crowded airport concourse to security, onlookers gawked as I passed by. Unlike me, these strangers hadn't had months to adjust to my startling appearance. Nevertheless, I felt hurt by the intrusive gawks, and I would have given anything not to look and feel like I did. I deeply missed the woman that I was before the crash.

Beige Tubigrip covered my arms and hid the sterile white gauze bandages that protected my open wounds. The tips of my deformed fingers emerged from the black pressurized gloves on my hands. The fire had destroyed most of my fingernails. Existing nail remnants were painted with a bright-red nail polish for Christmas, as were my toenails. Wearing nail polish was one of the few things I could do to feel feminine. Melissa told me that when I was in a coma, she had painted my toenails. My feet were among the few parts of my body not burned. Only my right pinky toe had a slight burn where my tennis shoe had melted. My toenails and ankles were intact. Thick white tennis socks had protected them from the flash burn.

We approached security at Concourse B. Only six people were ahead of us. Melissa placed our carry-on bags in the plastic trays, and we walked through the security clearance without any delay.

My skirt and soft blouse hid the spandex-like, custom pressure stockings and vest I had to wear. The stockings helped to relieve the bizarre stinging, tingling nerve-ending sensations; regulated blood flow through my legs to minimize swelling; and were supposed to reduce scarring. The tight stockings increased circulation, so they made me feel warmer. A Uvex plastic mask with four beige straps to secure it onto my head covered my red, disfigured face except for two elliptical-shaped holes for my eyes, two straw-sized holes in the sculpted nose that allowed air to pass through to my nostrils, and a tiny oval opening about an inch wide for my mouth. I had to wear the mask night and day, except when I ate, washed my face, or showered. It was supposed to reduce the formation of hypertrophic (raised, red) scars. The mask was hot and uncomfortable and triggered more unwanted attention.

But I was headed home for Christmas. So I resolved not to allow the stares to upset me.

As we made our way to the gate, I recalled occasions before the accident when, in busy airports, handsome men did double takes to flirt with me. They used to be eager to meet and talk with me. That day, they abruptly turned their heads or looked down toward the floor to avoid making eye contact with me. Their reaction reminded me that I would probably never experience an intimate relationship with a man. Quickly, I pushed this negative thought out of my mind and focused on the trip ahead.

I longed to see family and friends. I had discovered a feeling of comfort with people who knew me before the accident. I didn't have to prove my worth to old acquaintances and family members. Strangers did not realize that I had been a successful executive and treated me as if I were "less than" others and didn't have talent, skills, and abilities. I had lost the hard-earned "equity" in myself that I had built as an accomplished executive. Friends and family appreciated all I had endured and remembered the woman I was. I didn't have to use physical and emotional energy to explain what had happened and relive all the angst associated with the accident.

As I waited to board the plane, my thoughts returned to the trip ahead. I imagined entering the hunter-green front door of my mom's modest, white, wood-frame house and inhaling the aromas of sweet potatoes with marshmallows, brown sugar, and cinnamon baking in the oven, freshly cooked yellow squash with onions, mashed potatoes, homemade pumpkin pie, fudge, and her famous vanilla pound cake.

I envisioned sitting in my favorite rocking chair, with the swan-neck arms and a throw with a black-and-white cow motif. Melissa and I had combined our resources one year to have this custom rocker made for Mom. Mom's house had cow memorabilia everywhere. She grew up on a dairy farm; throughout her life, friends and family gave her various cow-themed gifts. She had a cow soap dish, a kitchen-sink cow stopper, cow doorstops, and cow pictures, curtains, area rugs, sugar bowl, creamer, and more. Whenever I see cows on anything, I smile and think of Mom.

An exquisite, antique, oak china cabinet sat in Mom's small, bright dining room. Encased behind original glass panels were irreplaceable crystal and china keepsakes that used to belong to my grandmothers. Mom's forget-me-not china belonged to her stepmother, Pauline. Mom didn't have even one keepsake from her mother, who had died of malnutrition when Mom was only three years old. Sometimes she cried just thinking about this.

I thought about sipping a glass of champagne or wine from one of her elegant, embossed crystal glasses. I remembered many times gathered around Mom's kitchen table while sharing meals, talking, laughing, and celebrating special occasions.

The gate attendant announced, "All those with children or who need additional assistance may board now." Unwillingly, I now qualified for this group, so Melissa and I walked down the ramp to board the plane. My pulse quickened as we approached the entrance to the aircraft, partly from excitement and partly from anxiety. I wasn't afraid of flying, because I knew and believed the statistics. It was much safer to travel by air than by car. But I was concerned that the experience, the sound of the engines, or the smell of fuel might trigger a panic attack. In addition, I was apprehensive that I might feel claustrophobic once the cabin doors were closed and locked.

From my previous work as a flight attendant, I knew that the most significant risk of a crash occurred during takeoff and landing, so once we were in the air, I sighed in relief. We were in the bulkhead seats. I preferred being as close to the front of the plane as possible, so I wouldn't feel claustrophobic. The flight attendants were attentive and friendly. One of them came over and said, "Do you mind if I ask what happened to you?"

"No, not at all. I was burned in a private-airplane crash in the Bahamas."

"Oh my God, you are so lucky to be alive. When did it happen?"

"Nine months ago. This is the first time I've flown since."

"Was anyone else injured in the crash?"

This question was the one that I most dreaded answering. "Yes, my fiancé, Roger, died due to injuries from the crash."

"Oh, I'm so sorry. You've been through a lot, haven't you?"

I appreciated her acknowledgment of my suffering and loss and her sincerity.

"We recently lost several of our dearest friends and colleagues in the crash of Flight 427 when it nose-dived into the ground just outside Pittsburgh as it was preparing to land. You probably heard about it. A crash of any aircraft awakens old memories and anxieties. Well, I better get back to work. Just let me know if you need anything, okay?"

"Thank you. So sorry about the loss of your friends and colleagues."

Talking with the flight attendant made the time pass quickly. Although we were seated in the coach section, we received first-class service from the compassionate crew.

From the cockpit, the captain announced, "Prepare the cabin for landing." The flight attendants delivered words I knew by rote but that were now tinged with anxiety: "Please buckle your seat belts and return all tray tables to the upright position." I took a deep breath, closed my eyes, asked God to give us a safe landing, and waited for the tires to touch the tarmac. A smooth, perfect landing! I had faced my fear.

We saw Mom and Hal waving as we approached the baggage claim area. They made their way through the crowd of holiday travelers and greeted us with smiles and hugs. "How was your flight?" Hal asked.

"The flight attendants treated us like VIPs," I said.

"Well, that's because you are VIPs!"

Hal and Melissa loaded our bags into Mom's Honda Accord, and we headed for home. I felt happy but worn out from the travel and preparations. Mom's miniature poodle, Binky, greeted us with a wagging tale and whimpers. Apparently, Binky didn't mind my changed appearance. As I walked into my bedroom, tears welled in my eyes. I realized how lucky and blessed I was to be alive and felt grateful that I had lived so much of my life intact. I had known the exhilaration of being loved, adored, and appreciated for my intellect and capabilities. I had traveled extensively and enjoyed many athletic endeavors. Had I been burned earlier, I might not have had many divine experiences and opportunities. There was a comfort in knowing that I likely had more of my life behind me than before me.

Over the next few days, Ruth, a physical therapist who was one of my favorite aunts, stopped by to visit me. She led me through some exercises and range-of-motion routines, lifting my arms and rotating my wrists. I felt comfortable with Aunt Ruth. She grasped the depth of my injury and losses and reassured me that someday I would be able to function with few limitations. Throughout her distinguished career, she had worked with many severely impaired individuals. I valued her expertise and opinion.

Most of my visitors were overcome with emotion when they saw me for the first time. Tears rolled down their faces, and some placed a hand to their mouth in disbelief. They had never seen someone so severely burned before, and they remembered what I used to look like before the crash.

Before my injury

Almost everyone reminded me that they had prayed for my recovery. All had sent cards. I'd even received cards from people who had heard about the accident but whom I'd never met.

My room growing up was on the house's front side. During this visit, I took the back bedroom because I could get in and out of bed more easily in this room. Mom's small house was bright and cheerful, full of energy, and, truth be told, too much chaos for me. Terrified of being burned again, I was uneasy about staying in the house because of the gas heat. I was afraid to be anywhere near a flame or fire. Just the smell of smoke escalated a cascade of anxiety. Mom loved wood-burning fires, and on Christmas Eve, we had always lit the fireplace in the living room—but not that year. Although she couldn't fully understand my fear, she respected my wishes.

Instead, we gathered around the fragrant, live Christmas tree and opened one gift each. As usual, Melissa wore her Santa Claus hat and distributed the gifts. We sipped Kahlúa and cream and ate some of Mom's delicious pound cake. Mom had long ago given up on buying gifts for me. She knew I preferred to select my own presents, so I always looked forward to a gift certificate. Melissa, on the other hand, loved to shop for gifts.

Traveling home to Greensboro and spending Christmas with Mom, family, and friends was an important milestone. Only twice had I ever missed being with Mom at Christmastime, once when Roger and I had traveled to France with two other couples and another time when we had joined the same friends on a holiday skiing trip to Beaver Creek. Both times, I had felt guilty about not being with Mom and Melissa, and it hadn't felt like Christmas without them. I had vowed not to miss another Christmas with them. However, fate, destiny, or terrible luck had almost prevented me from being with them this Christmas. I believed there was only one reason I had lived: God had spared my life. Although I didn't know why, I firmly thought that I was alive for a purpose. This belief was at the core of my strength and determination to fight to regain my independence and a productive life. My body had been crucified, but my faith and perseverance had been restored.

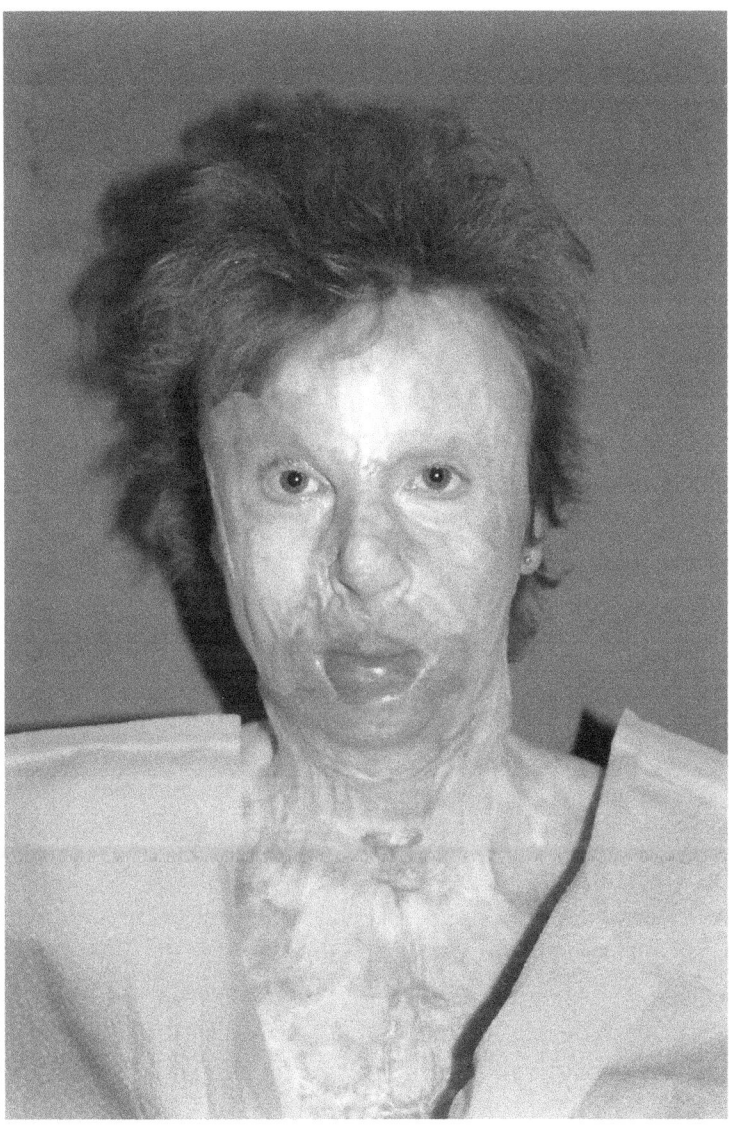

One year after the accident

CHAPTER THIRTEEN

Going Solo

You can't go back and make a new start, but you can start right now and make a brand new ending.

James R. Sherman

Two years after the crash

April arrived, and as I had hoped, I was headed to Nashville, Tennessee, to attend the ABA conference and to finally meet Alan and Delwyn. For more than a week, Melissa had helped me gather and compactly pack my clothes and wound care supplies. Unfortunately, I was too weak to manage or lift a heavy suitcase. In addition, I had reserved a car service in Nashville, as I knew I'd need help with my bags.

Traveling alone in my condition was simultaneously exciting and nerve-racking. Still, I wanted to prove to myself that I could do it. I had gained a few pounds and walked farther daily without a cane. With greater strength came the confidence that I could manage on my own. It wouldn't be easy, but I believed that it was possible.

Melissa drove me to the airport. She pulled over to the curb, unloaded my suitcases from the trunk, and rolled them to the ticketing agent. As we parted, she said, "Call me the minute you arrive at the hotel. I'll be a nervous wreck until I know that you're okay. Have a great time, be careful, and don't overdo it. I love you." Her serious expression conveyed her concern. She gave me a hug and watched as I walked toward the doors to the terminal.

I turned around, smiled, and waved goodbye. I had always been comfortable in airport terminals and found them fascinating. All sorts of people were either excited to arrive or saddened to depart. Yet I knew that this trip held unique challenges I would have to meet head-on. As I walked through the terminal, I felt many eyes on me. I was dressed in a cotton sleeveless turtleneck top and my favorite gold ankle-length skirt. And, of course, my ever-present beige pressure garments. My black pressure gloves looked like something Michael Jackson would have liked. I opted not to wear my plastic facial mask, to draw less attention.

As I walked down the crowded corridor, people stared like I was the star of a horror film. Their jaws dropped, their eyes bulged, and their eyebrows raised in shock. Some diverted their attention to the floor, and some gasped in disbelief. Some whispered, "Oh my God, look at that poor woman."

These reactions reinforced my determination to stand tall. I refused to be diminished by their stares. Head held high, I kept walking toward my gate, my proud stride frequently interrupted by my need to rest and rearrange my pocketbook and carry-on. I'd tried to eliminate the extra suitcase, but there were specific medical supplies and personal items that I had to keep with me in case my checked bag was lost.

At the gate, I had to board with those with special

needs—there was no way I'd be able to stow my carry-on on my own.

Then, once the flight attendant closed the door and locked the escape slide into position, I felt a surge of anxiety and claustrophobia. I closed my eyes and breathed slowly and deeply. I prayed: *God, please watch over and guide the pilot and crew, and let us have a safe, uneventful flight to Nashville.*

The plane bounced, bumped, creaked down the tarmac, and slowly lifted off into the blue sky. Relieved, I diverted my attention to my book and contemplated what would be next.

I'd never been to Nashville before, but I had always enjoyed traveling to new places and discovering the unique characteristics of various cities and towns. I wondered if Nashville would resemble Memphis. I had lived in Memphis as a child. Like most people, the main thing I remembered about Memphis was that Elvis Presley had a home there. My mother always got a kick out of telling people that Elvis had kissed me. Once, he stopped in front of our yard on the way to check on his horses. I was dressed in my bathing suit and wore a pair of silver sparkly play high heels, the kind that you can buy at service stations. Mom had asked me why I was dressed like this, and I had told her, "I'm waiting for Elvis." This turned out to be my lucky day because he noticed me and stopped. He got out of his truck, stooped down to say hello, lifted me up to his face, and kissed me on the cheek. I was thrilled to be kissed by the future king of rock 'n' roll. Elvis was on the cusp of becoming a national celebrity at the time. He already had won the hearts of the local females in our neighborhood, who eagerly awaited just a glimpse of this handsome, sexy hometown hunk. My mom was a starstruck, devoted fan. Once, I'd bought front-row tickets for her to see him perform in person. She described the experience as sheer ecstasy. The thought of this made me smile.

In minutes, we would be landing. I stashed my book back

inside my bag, cinched my seat belt tighter, and glanced out the window for a peek of the patchwork countryside as the plane descended. The plane touched down gently. The flight attendant retrieved my bag from the overhead compartment, and I exited the aircraft. Walking down the corridor, I saw a young Black man dressed in a suit and tie holding a placard with my last name. As I approached him, I smiled and introduced myself. He was a little taken aback by my appearance but adjusted quickly.

"Welcome to Nashville, Ms. Pell. Do you have more luggage?"

"Yes, I have one other bag. A purple-and-red ribbon tied to the handle will help you to identify it." I struggled to keep pace with his stride. My suitcase was one of the first to show up on the conveyor. Outside the terminal, he loaded the bags into a black Lincoln Town Car, and we headed to Opryland.

When we arrived, I saw the building towering so high into the sky that its size made me nervous. Inside, the place was the size of a small town! The lobby was bustling with crowds of people I would have to push through and possibly bump against just to check into my room. I kept the meeting with Alan uppermost in my mind. There was no turning back now—I could do this. Exhausted from the travel, I then had to wait in a long line to check in. When I had first decided to attend the conference, I contemplated asking Melissa to accompany me to help, but I wanted to prove I could be okay on my own. At that moment, I wished I had given in to reason instead of pride.

Once inside the hotel, I couldn't understand why surgeons, nurses, rehabilitation specialists, and others weren't more cordial. I was disappointed and confused by their reaction to me. Unbeknownst to me, the burn care professionals looked forward to attending the ABA conference to enjoy a break from the bedside care of burn patients. One nurse said that the last thing she wanted to see was another "melted face."

I felt like an uninvited guest at a party. Of all places, I thought I would be embraced by this group, not shunned. But maybe I was also a painful reminder of the inadequacies in burn care.

Although I had done many walking exercises, I knew this day would push me beyond my previous limits. Resolved to make this a positive experience, I followed the bellman to my room. I was relieved to be at the hotel and to have someone else manage my luggage. Terrified of being trapped in a fire, I'd reserved a room close to the emergency exits. Just to reach my room, I had to walk farther than I'd walked all at once since the crash.

Once I was settled in my room and unpacked, I called Alan to arrange to meet him and Delwyn for dinner. We agreed on six o'clock. That was perfect; I could stop by the registration tables for the conference on my way to meet them. I left my room at 5:15 to allow plenty of time to find my way. Walking down the main corridor toward the registration area, I noticed a petite, professionally dressed female burn survivor with facial differences walking alongside a slender, tall man.

She wore a dark-colored, stylish wig. Despite her scars, she was attractive. As they approached me, I expected her to smile and greet me, but to my surprise, she whispered something to her companion and ignored me. Hurt and confused, I was stunned. Even a burn survivor was treating me like a leper.

On my way, I passed groups of individuals wearing badges that identified them as being with the conference. Shockingly, none of them spoke to me. Given the "unwelcome" I was receiving, I was especially eager to connect with Alan and Delwyn, as I knew I could count on their warm reception. By that time, I needed some positive reinforcement.

As I approached the restaurant, I instantly recognized

Alan. I was so excited to finally see this man face to face. From his voice, I envisioned a tall, charismatic, well-dressed, and, perhaps, even commanding, man.

Despite extensive facial scars and an unusual blue right eye, he was a formidable, elegant man, even dressed in denim jeans, a western shirt with a silver bolo tie, and snakeskin cowboy boots. He radiated warmth as he extended his hand and said, "You must be Charlene."

His white hairpiece was attractive and didn't entirely cover his melted earlobes. His eyes sparkled. I was surprised that he was tanned. He looked timeless, although I knew he was in his late sixties. There wasn't a wrinkle on his taut skin. He was utterly at ease and confident.

"Welcome, dear. It's so wonderful to finally meet you in person. This is my wife, Delwyn." Without hesitation, she stepped forward to hug me as if we were old friends.

"How was your flight, dear?"

"Just the way that I prefer them to be—uneventful."

"Come, let's get seated so we can get acquainted."

Her accent, I would learn, signaled that she was from New Zealand. Petite and with short hair just beginning to gray, she had a cute, upturned nose and appeared younger than Alan. She looked like a seasoned conference attendee, dressed in a navy pantsuit and wearing comfortable shoes.

It did not take long to get to know one another as we ordered our food and ate. They discussed all the activities they expected to do while at the conference and invited me to join them for each one.

We talked for nearly two hours, and I learned that they and their one assistant, Ruth, were operating the Phoenix Society. They constantly worked, responding to requests for referrals, resources, and information or coordinating burn camps, conferences, support groups, and more. Unfortunately,

the organization was in dire need of financial and physical resources to meet increasing demand.

Delwyn said, "We converted the upstairs of the house into
office space to accommodate the organization."

Alan and Delwyn wrote the quarterly newsletter. I was astonished by their commitment and dedication to the advance-
ment of aftercare for burn survivors. The Phoenix Society
had become their life. Delwyn had been recognized by Queen
Elizabeth for her efforts to enrich the lives of burn survivors,
one of whom was Delwyn's son. She and Alan made a dynamic
couple.

After being with them, I knew I wanted to help them and
the organization.

The ABA conference, on the other hand, proved to be one
disappointment after another. The segment for burn survivors
titled "Psychosocial Issues" was devoid of any information to
help a survivor recover emotionally or psychologically from a
burn injury. Of all things, the session was about writing grants!
I was appalled, even more so when I saw that the woman who
had snubbed me was the presenter. Not one lecture addressed
any psychological, social, or emotional issues important to a
survivor after discharge from the hospital.

I discovered that many of the members of the ABA did
not believe that they had any responsibility to provide psychosocial programs to help survivors adjust to their changed
appearances, endure grief and loss, or deal with issues related
to reentering society and the workplace. I was astonished. The
Phoenix Society and a handful of other regional burn-related
nonprofits were the only sources of peer support, education,
resources, and advocacy for burn survivors and their families.
I couldn't believe the appalling lack of aftercare programs to
help survivors with these issues.

It seemed inconceivable to me that many burn surgeons and doctors didn't feel any responsibility for patients'

adjustment and well-being after discharge. Children were the exception. There were several burn camps exclusively for children throughout the States. Ironically, the same health care professionals who recognized that children needed additional support were oblivious to the vast need expressed by adults. I wondered how they could possibly think that patients with dramatically altered, disfigured physical appearances, emotional and psychological challenges, loss of identity, physical challenges, grief issues, and work-related losses could recover and reintegrate into society and the workplace without professional intervention.

The nurses, occupational therapists, and physical therapists seemed most attuned to survivors' emotional and psychological needs. They were primarily the professionals who volunteered their time and talents at burn camps, alongside firefighters.

Firefighters were revered at these meetings, and many sessions were devoted to their needs. Firefighters had raised millions of dollars to fund some of the hospitals' research, programs, and equipment. The ABA worked closely with the International Association of Fire Fighters (IAFF) to advocate for legislation to reduce and prevent burn injuries. Unfortunately, burn survivors themselves were only tolerated at the conference.

Fortunately, I did enjoy one other pleasant experience at the ABA conference. I ate dinner with one of the surgeons who had saved my life, Dr. Michael Peck. I was a hero to him and the rest of the burn care team at Jackson Memorial Hospital. Dr. Peck encouraged me to get involved with the Phoenix Society. Clearly, he recognized the need for improvements in aftercare.

Getting to know Alan and Delwyn and learning about the critical work of the Phoenix Society made the arduous trip worthwhile. I left the conference firmly committed to dedicating the rest of my life to working with burn survivors and others with facial disfigurement. Alan and Delwyn emphasized the critical need for fundraising to continue existing programs that provided essential peer support and information to survivors worldwide, so I vowed to use my skills in this area to help raise money for the society. Previously, I had raised thousands of dollars for charitable causes.

Maybe I, too, could be a voice to help other burn survivors. My former work throughout the years prepared me well for this new role. I felt like I had a new purpose. I was energized and eager to learn everything I could about the psychosocial issues facing burn survivors and the available programs and resources.

Attending this conference was a monumental milestone in my recovery. On the flight home, I thought of ideas to help with fundraising and programming. I offered to write the upcoming solicitation letter and made notes. The organization's next World Burn Congress (WBC) was going to be in Detroit in October. I was eager to attend this conference because there would be hundreds of burn survivors, family members, and health care providers. And, unlike at the ABA conference, the workshops would focus on survivors' concerns.

Often Alan and Delwyn communicated with me by phone or email. I wanted to use my skills to advance burn care, and I believed I could contribute in this area and be a voice to advocate for burn survivors.

I researched and read every book by or for a burn survivor that I could find, trying to learn about this field and about disfigurement and staring. In addition, I joined the ABA and discovered another organization, called the Southern Medical Association, that presented an annual conference for the burn centers located in the southern region.

Alan and Delwyn were eager for me to attend the WBC so they could introduce me to the burn survivors community. Alan was contemplating retirement.

In June, after our meeting at the ABA conference, he called. "Delwyn and I would love to have you lead the society once we retire."

"I'm honored that you would entrust me with your amazing organization. I would love to help, but I have years more of surgery and rehab. Right now, I couldn't devote my full attention and energy to managing and seeking funding to maintain and grow the charity. Let me think about it."

I was excited about the prospect of this opportunity yet concerned that I wouldn't be able to dedicate a hundred percent of my time to an organization that was in serious need of funding to sustain operations. Importantly, I had to have health insurance to cover ongoing reconstructive and plastic surgery. It would be very risky to accept the offer.

Meanwhile, I thought about ways to raise money for the Phoenix Society. Annually, DCOTA hosted a successful sample sale where we opened to the public for just a weekend. I asked my boss, Joan, if I could approach some of the showrooms about donating a portion of the proceeds from the sale to the Phoenix Society. She agreed, and several showrooms participated. I contacted the director of development at the University of Miami's Jackson Memorial Hospital and invited her to participate.

Early on a Saturday morning in August, we met at DCOTA, set up a tabletop display in the atrium showcasing the work of the Burn Center and the Phoenix Society, and distributed brochures and flyers to the shoppers. One of the showrooms donated a beautiful rug as a raffle prize, and we sold tickets for $10. We divided the $5,000 that we raised between the Burn Center and the Phoenix Society.

I asked friends and relatives to make donations to the Phoenix Society, instead of sending me gifts for birthdays and Christmas. Every waking moment, I thought about ways to sustain and enhance the Phoenix Society.

CHAPTER FOURTEEN

Something to Talk About

One needs something to believe in, something for which one can have whole-hearted enthusiasm. One needs to feel that one's life has meaning, that one is needed in this world.

Hannah Senesh

Summer of 1996

Chris said, "Char, we want you to be in our wedding." A public event? I clenched my teeth. Didn't she realize what I was going through, how self-conscious I felt about my disfigured appearance?

"What do you want me to do?" I said quietly, looking up at her from my desk.

"We want you to read a passage from Hebrew scripture, the Song of Songs. It's about a couple's longing for each other." How long ago that seemed—a couple's longing for each other. I could only fantasize about what that would feel like.

"Uh, that sounds intense. Let me read through it and see if I can do it."

"Jim and I talked about this last night. We really want you to read this with our friend Bill."

Jim was a former priest who had left the church after deep contemplation so that he could marry Chris, one of my associates at DCOTA. He was eager to marry Chris, and they had planned an outdoor wedding in Secret Woods Nature Center, a wilderness park in Dania Beach.

I was excited to be asked to participate in the wedding but hesitant because of my appearance. I went home and read through the passage several times. It was exceptionally sensual for scripture from the Bible.

One verse read: "Let him kiss me with the kisses of his mouth. Your love is more delightful than wine."

I called Chris and told her I couldn't do it. "It feels awkward for someone who looks like me to read something so sensual. Sure, I remember what it used to feel like to be sexy, but I barely feel feminine anymore." Standing next to Jim's best friend, Bill—a tall, handsome man—while thinking about the raised, red scars on my face, neck, and chest, I expected that it would be difficult for me to express the couple's feelings in the Song of Songs.

"Char, you're the perfect person to read this. The only one! Please do it for us. Read it a few times. It will become easier. I'm sure."

I didn't want to disappoint Chris. Although we were primarily colleagues from work, she and Jim had been very kind to me, and they had gone through so much to get to this point in their relationship. I wanted to fulfill their seemingly simple request. She was also one of several coworkers who had donated blood for my many transfusions.

"Okay, I'll give it a try." I hung up the phone and walked over to the glass sliding doors to the balcony. I recalled the evenings after work when Roger and I had lingered on our balcony until dusk, sipping margaritas and talking about our day. The song "I'll Be Seeing You" popped into my mind and caused tears in my eyes. Before the crash, I had been learning how to play this melody on the piano. Under normal circumstances, the song had caused me to become very emotional. After the crash, it was nearly impossible to stop the gush of tears from my eyes whenever I heard the song. My feelings reminded me of what it felt like to long for someone. I would need to draw upon these feelings to rouse the emotion to read the Song of Songs passage at the wedding.

I rehearsed this scripture as if I were auditioning for a role in a Broadway play. I practiced my lines while standing in front of the bathroom vanity mirror, cooking dinner, and driving to work.

"'Let him kiss me with the kisses of his mouth. Your love is more delightful than wine; Delicate is the fragrance of your perfume; Your name is an oil poured out.'" I recorded the reading to listen to it while driving or preparing for bed or work. I changed my tone and volume for emphasis, paused for effect, and varied my pace to accentuate the most profound phrases.

On the evening of the wedding, I found a quiet spot tucked away from the guests, closed my eyes, and prayed, "Lord, please give me the composure to deliver this passage with passion and confidence."

As Chris and Jim looked on in the magical twilight, Bill and I stood, faced one another, and read our parts.

Bill said, "'You ravish my heart, my sister, my promised bride; you ravish my heart with a single one of your glances, with one pearl of your necklace. What spells lie in your love, my sister, my promised bride!'"

"'Awake, north wind, come, wind of the south! Breathe

over my garden, to spread its sweet smell around. Let my beloved come into his garden, let him taste its rarest fruits,'" I said.

A gentle breeze blew across my face as I embraced each word and delivered it confidently. Years of speaking in front of staff, at conferences, and in sales presentations had given me some comfort with public speaking. But my disfigurement had stolen a bit of my confidence. Nevertheless, a sense of satisfaction and relief flowed over me once I completed my part. I had faced my fear and succeeded.

After the service, Bill said, "Wow, you put your heart and soul in your delivery. You were terrific!"

"Thanks, I really practiced a lot. I'm just glad it's over."

One afternoon after the wedding, I retrieved the mail and found a lovely note from Jim and Chris. They wrote, "You were poised, prepared, and you were perfect with a voice that had passion, power, and pure poetry, as that reading called for!" I smiled with delight. Chris and Jim also acknowledged that they knew it took lots of inner strength to read the passage.

Shortly after Chris and Jim's wedding, a priest who had attended the ceremony asked me to give a homily at three masses at St. Maurice Catholic Church. I didn't know what a homily was until I read the definition. I grew up attending a Methodist church; however, I had attended mass many times with my best friend from high school, Peggy.

I agreed to speak and spent weeks writing, editing, and rehearsing my speech, titled "A Second Chance." In the speech, I shared that prior to the accident, I had become agnostic. I had strayed from my faith because I didn't understand how a loving God could allow so much pain, misery, and violence into our broken world. I saw good, faithful people suffer and die, innocent children starve of malnutrition, catastrophic events that killed thousands, and a society that appeared to be losing its morals and values. I wondered, Where was God? I told the audience, "I put my trust in the one person I could count on all the time, myself. I thought that I could overcome anything on my own." Foolishly, I thought I was in control of my life and destiny.

In seconds, my life had been upended and catastrophically changed. Lying in a hospital bed, unable to move or speak, I had quickly realized that my faith and fortitude were the only things in life that couldn't be taken away from me. Fervently, I believed that God had spared me from death. Realistically, considering the site and conditions of the crash, it should have been impossible to escape the flames—and yet, miraculously, we had escaped.

Often, we read about people who turn to God after a tragic accident. Why? For some of us, it is the only possible condition that could force us to relinquish the control we exercise in our daily lives. Despite years of listening to positive motivational speakers, reading self-help books, and doing everything imaginable to be successful, healthy, prosperous, and secure, I discovered that my destiny is not in my control.

The cathedral venue was much larger, more formal, and more intimidating than the wedding site. So the day before I was scheduled to speak, I asked the priest if I could visit the place where I'd be speaking, to familiarize myself with the setting. Doing this would make me feel more at ease on the day of the homily.

Despite the visit and rigorous preparation and practice, I wondered if anyone could see my shaking legs as I approached the podium. After just a few words, my mouth became parched. I took a sip of water and continued: "If this hadn't happened to me, I would never have connected to the amazing people and purpose that God had in store for me. God used a crisis to change the direction of my life. He had to use a crisis to get my attention." At the time of the accident, I had been living with the mindset of "live fast, love hard, and die young."

I worked long hours and drank more than I should have. Unintentionally, I was risking too much for myself and others. After each mass, I stood outside, next to the priest, and greeted all the guests. One woman cried as she gave me a rosary that she had been given in Guatemala. Another woman said, "I called my husband to tell him that he had to get dressed to come and hear you at the next service. Your message was so important and touched so many people." That was the moment that I realized God's plan for my life.

I was reminded of the comforting words in a letter from my mom's favorite pastor, Bob Miller. He wrote, "I do not believe that God brings bad things into our lives. But I do believe this, 'We know that all things work together for good for those who love God' (Romans 8:28). God brought eternal life through the evil that was imposed upon Jesus. . . . God has brought much good out of the tragedy of your life and God will continue to do good work in and through you."

CHAPTER FIFTEEN

Scent of a Man

What is now proved was once only imagined.

William Blake

Two and a half years after the crash

Everywhere I looked, I saw burn survivors, some with facial burns, some missing fingers, hands, arms, or legs. There were people with prosthetic arms and legs. Many of the guys were bald or wearing hairpieces. They were laughing and talking like ordinary people gathered for a special occasion.

I was in Detroit at the welcome reception for the Phoenix Society's WBC. That night, I could fit in.

As many burn survivors reconnected with friends and exchanged hugs, it reminded me of a high school reunion. I spotted a small opening at the crowded bar and made my way there to order a glass of wine. Before the bartender could deliver the wine, a slender, tan male survivor dressed in faded jeans and a crisp, white button-down collared shirt welcomed me. "Hi, I'm David. Can I get you a drink?"

"Oh, thanks, but I just ordered a glass of wine."

It had been a long time since a man had offered to buy me a drink. Since my injury, I avoided bars.

A fit woman in her early twenties leaned against a pillar. She wore snug-fitting jeans and a top that revealed her scarred midriff. How could she expose her disfigurement so easily? She was smiling and chatting with some young guys. I asked David, "Do you know that young woman over there? She seems to be so comfortable with her burns."

"Oh, that's Chloe. She's a sweetheart. She's very involved with the Phoenix Society. She volunteers to help with the burn camps for children. She was burned when she was only three years old. I think one of her brothers was responsible for starting the fire, but I'm not sure. She'd be happy to talk with you."

Chloe must never have known any other kind of skin or appearance. After hearing her story, I felt fortunate to have been burned at an older age. I'd lived many years of my life as an attractive, desirable woman, my privilege and my torment. But even with severe scars, Chloe was alluring and pretty.

Later, as people loosened up, Chloe moved to the rhythm of the music, her hips swaying in a sexy, seductive way. My own sense of sexuality had been shattered. For months, I had felt androgynous, with no hope of ever having an intimate relationship again, but after watching this cute girl move so sensuously, I thought, *If she can do this, then so can I.*

A thin, young woman wearing a turban approached me. I was taken back by her appearance, as she had two small holes in her face where her nose should have been. I focused my attention on her brown eyes to talk to her.

"Hi, I'm Rachel. Is this your first time here?"

"Yes, how about you?"

"It's my second time. I came last year. It was wonderful. I vowed to never miss another one. Everyone is so nice and helpful. Here, I feel like an ordinary person. I don't have to deal with stares and taunting. Everyone here understands what I am going through."

Rachel had been burned in a gas explosion upon entering her home. Everything had been destroyed. Thankfully, her husband was at work, and her son was at school. She was still in the process of healing, with more surgeries required to restore her nose and ears. Her husband had left her. He couldn't cope with her changed appearance and challenges. For now, her mother was helping her care for her son.

Even with my pronounced disfigurement, I found it difficult to concentrate while talking to Rachel and other survivors with facial burns. It was physically challenging to maintain eye contact, as if I was trying to manually adjust the focus on a camera as my eyes and brain competed for dominance.

It was also difficult to absorb and process so much emotional pain and anguish as I listened to their stories.

The experience and insight were helping me to appreciate and consider the rapid adjustments "normal-looking" people must make to talk with me and other people with facial differences. Perhaps they, too, sometimes felt overcome with emotion by our appearance.

Unable to stand for long periods, I looked around for a place to sit. A thoughtful survivor offered me a barstool. He told me he had lost his wife and three children in a horrific automobile accident.

Each person had a tragic story of loss and suffering, yet they were engaged and enjoying the interaction with others. Although I would not have expected this, I felt almost "normal" in their presence, which allowed me to feel comfortable in this fellowship of survivors, caregivers, and burn care professionals.

Before leaving the reception, I spoke with Julie, a woman who had lost all four of her children in a mobile-home fire caused by faulty wiring. I winced just contemplating such an unimaginable, heartbreaking loss and fought to hold back the tears pooling in my eyes as she told me about the fire. She was consumed with guilt and grief, clinging to the hope that she could somehow find the strength and courage to go on without her children.

Back in my room, I perused the program, tortured by the choices between sessions on family relationships, adult survivors burned as children, intimacy, pain management, posttraumatic stress disorder, and other vital issues. I needed to learn how to live fully and freely with my disfigurement and challenges.

There were support groups for survivors, family members, and burn care professionals. Physicians, nurses, psychologists, and social workers were on hand to share insights for overcoming the challenges specific to burn injuries. I was so excited about the evening and the days ahead that I couldn't fall asleep. I was eager for morning to arrive.

*

There was one session I was determined not to miss—the intimacy session. How candid would the panelists be? Would they share how they gained the confidence to expose their disfigured bodies to a partner? Did they describe hidden burns, to prepare their partner beforehand? Did they explain that their skin felt different to the touch because of the burns or ask their partner to avoid touching certain areas sensitive to stroking? Did other survivors' skin fluctuate in temperature and color depending on the location and depth of the burn? So many thoughts and questions were swirling in my mind. Taking a long, deep breath, I tried to calm my anxiety and divert my attention to the panel moderator as she said, "Welcome, everyone. We encourage you to share your thoughts and experiences. We all can learn from each other; don't be shy. If you're thinking it, someone else probably is, too." A microphone was set up in the aisle for that purpose.

More than fifty people were packed into the room, and to get a seat, I had to slide past a few. As I took my seat, I noticed the missing arm and prosthetic of the man beside me. In front of me, there was a woman with a wig. To my left was a young man with extensive burns, including on his face. Like me, were they seeking reassurance that despite their disfigurement, love and intimacy remained a possibility? I wondered if anyone from the audience would be willing to ask a question on this particular topic in front of so many people.

I crossed my legs and caught a glimpse of my gold-and-silver anklet. Wearing it made me feel feminine. My legs used to be beautiful; they had been toned and shapely. Now they looked like shapeless, scarred sticks bound by flesh-colored pressure garments. There would never be anything sexy about my legs, but I was grateful to have legs. It seemed impossible to me that any man could ever feel attracted to me. I clung to the hope that maybe the panelists might convince me otherwise. I leaned forward on my chair, eager to hear what the panelists and others would say.

One of the panelists, an attractive woman in her thirties who had hidden burns caused by a bath that had been too hot, led the way. She bravely recounted her story, describing a broad range of emotions to which we all could relate: Trepidation about the first time she was intimate. Her fear of rejection. Whether she should tell her partner about her scars beforehand. Wondering if he would be repulsed by her scars. She had decided to tell her partner, to avoid an awkward situation. In her case, he was very understanding and still found her to be desirable and attractive. Her partner helped her to become more comfortable with her disfiguring burns.

Another woman with severe burns on her face and much of her body said she dimmed the lights in the bedroom before she and her partner began to make love. They had become good friends before becoming intimate, so they cared about one another. She emphasized that it was essential that we become comfortable with and accept our altered bodies to experience intimacy.

Others weren't so fortunate.

Unlike some of the panelists whose burns were hidden, mine were front and center, always on display. That had to make a difference. What man would ever be able to get beyond my appearance to get to know me, much less consider an intimate relationship?

On the one hand, I dreaded contemplating life devoid of touching, kissing, passion, or the ecstasy of orgasm. On the other, I couldn't imagine ever letting any man see me nude. It seemed impossible that any man whom I would find desirable could ever find me alluring in return. Whenever I had these thoughts, a line from George Gershwin's "But Not for Me" flashed through my mind. I didn't want to give up on being loved but had resigned myself, for now, to focusing on recovering and helping others.

Just a few weeks earlier, one of my favorite doctors had said, "Isn't it magnificent that your genitalia weren't burned. You can still have an orgasm!" At the time, stunned by his remark, I thought only a male doctor would think of this and be so brash as to say it!

I was covered in red raised scars from the top of my head to my breasts. Both legs were a snarl of tight, discolored, scarred skin from the top of my thighs to the tight bands around both ankles. That skin felt odd, like the texture of a thin latex glove. My abdomen and buttocks had been used as donor sites for skin to cover other parts of my body, so they, too, resembled pieces of a puzzle, with scars outlining the patterns of the donor sites.

Astonishingly, my red hair had grown back. That was a

blessing because, throughout the conference, I had noticed an attractive, middle-aged man named Alex who had my thoughts turning toward the possibility of intimacy. Earlier in the day, I had walked past him while he was smiling and laughing with friends. I spotted him as I entered the room for the session on sexuality. Even with extensive facial, neck, and arm burns, I found him to be charismatic, virile, and appealing. He moved with confidence and intent. His tender sage-green eyes and brown hair were a striking contrast against his scarred face. During one of the sessions, he described how he had been burned in a gas explosion. Engulfed by flames, he had managed to get out of the house. A neighbor heard the explosion, rushed to his side, and called 911. At one point, during an earlier session, we had traded a sympathetic glance.

Certainly, I couldn't be the only person whose libido hadn't given up on her.

There was only one way to know. In this semipublic setting, I'd have to get up and share my most intimate desires and fears. So, I approached the microphone, trying to think less about the eyes on my disfigured face and body and more about the ears tuned in to my heart, reminding myself that this was a welcoming community of other burn survivors.

With my gnarled hands clasped in front and legs shaking, I said, "At a wedding reception for a colleague from work, I was surprised when the groom asked me to dance. I felt his warm body close to me, his arms around me. It had been more than two years since I was close enough to a man to detect the scent of his cologne. I felt giddy as he held me close. I'm sure he had no idea of how he was affecting me, but it had been so long since I'd been held or touched by a man."

I had felt the same exhilaration as Al Pacino's character in the movie *Scent of a Woman*, where a retired, decorated lieutenant colonel, now blind, fulfills his wish to dance the sensuous tango with a beautiful woman. Pacino glided across the ballroom floor with a vivacious brunette gracefully following his every lead. He tucked his face into the nape of her neck and breathed in her captivating scent. His expression was ecstatic. I had felt the same giddy excitement. Dancing with the groom at the wedding had unearthed my desires as a woman, which I longed for. My voice quavered as I told the group, "I love to dance, and I miss dancing and the companionship of my fiancé. It deeply saddens me to think that I will probably never again experience love, romance, or passion." The audience was silent. Some were crying and wiping tears from their faces.

They knew.

By the end of the third day of the conference, I was tired and emotional yet encouraged and renewed. Most importantly, a spark of hope had me believing there was a possibility that I might someday experience a romantic relationship.

After the conclusion of the WBC, there was a banquet and dance. Having seen Chloe and others dance at the reception, I was ready to explore ways to get on the dance floor again. That started with my appearance, so I scheduled a consultation with Barbara Quayle, a burn survivor who was a makeup artist specializing in image enhancement for burn survivors. Although Barbara had no fingers on one hand and only a thumb and nubs on the other, she skillfully transformed my face by brushing on makeup that camouflaged and enhanced my discolored skin. Next, she matched a foundation to my skin color and showed me how to apply it with a wedge-shaped sponge. Then Barbara applied a translucent powder. Finally, she demonstrated how to create realistic-looking eyebrows, instead of the lines that I had drawn where my eyebrows used to appear. She said, "Remember, your eyebrows are sisters, not identical twins. They don't have to perfectly match."

She used a unique concealer and a lip liner to make my

enlarged lower lip appear smaller. She selected a flattering lip-stick color. I had tried many colors and needed something that didn't call too much attention to my lower lip.

Before being burned, I had preferred a natural, fresh look. After the consultation, I felt a bit too made up, yet Barbara's work highlighted my best feature, my hazel eyes.

I rushed up to my room to change clothes. My feet and ankles were so swollen that it was difficult to close the clasp on my black velvet Mary Jane slippers. I wore an outfit that I'd worn on a date with Roger to see Dionne Warwick. I had cho-sen to bring this ensemble because I could put it on by myself; it had no buttons or zippers. That night, I delighted in know-ing that the crossover bodice was flattering to my lean shape. I brushed my natural red hair, which had somehow regrown, and as I looked into the mirror one last time, I felt feminine and pretty in my own way.

Most of all, for the first time in more than two years, I felt like a woman hoping some man would ask me to dance.

As I entered the arch of balloons to the ballroom, Alex ap-proached me and said, "Would you like to join me for dinner?" A rush of adrenaline flooded my body just thinking about this.

"I would love to join you, but I've already promised to sit with Alan and Delwyn. They're expecting me. Let's connect after dinner and the presentation?"

He seemed disappointed but said, "Sure, that sounds good."

I had overheard some other women talking about this "available" guy during the conference, and I felt honored and excited that he seemed interested in getting to know me. I was eager to talk with him after dinner.

After the program, a DJ began to play some fantastic dance music. Rick Halpert, a trial attorney, came up beside me and said, "Let's dance, Char." Rick and his partners had repre-sented many burn survivors and were significant supporters of

the Phoenix Society. We often had talked during the conference. He pulled me close and whispered into my ear, "You will
experience love and romance again. Not everyone will, but, my
dear, you're an extraordinary woman, and there will be a man
out there who will recognize this and love you."

I smiled at just the thought of this. Of course, coming from
Rick, it meant the world to me. I wasn't certain that he would
be right, but for the first time since my injury, my mind had
opened to the possibility. He looked me in the eye and said,
"Char, it will happen." He spun and twirled me around the
dance floor. It was divine.

During this magical evening, it seemed as if almost every
guy in attendance asked me to dance! I felt like Cinderella at
the ball. Alex asked me to slow dance more than once. As he
pulled me close, I could feel the warmth of his muscular chest.
We barely moved from the same spot as he gently swayed me
back and forth.

After the banquet, we lingered in an alcove area near the
hotel elevators and talked for more than two hours. It was
nearly 1:00 a.m., and I had an early flight, so we had to say
good night. I sensed that, like me, he didn't want to end the
night. We hugged, and as I was about to walk away, he leaned
over and gently kissed me on my cheek.

"I'll give you a call in a few days," he said as we parted.
Then, reluctantly, we retired to our separate rooms.

Back in my room, I fantasized about what it would be like
to make love again. I was exhausted, and my feet were bleed-
ing. It was difficult to ignore all the thoughts racing through
my mind and the arousal in my body. I didn't want this night,
this feeling, or this event to end. It was exhilarating to be in
the company of others who understood my losses, challenges,
and desires. There, I was accepted and admired; outside, I was
an outcast.

The next day, I had to return to the real world, where I

wouldn't see another burn survivor until I went to the Burn Center at Jackson Memorial. But I was much better prepared to reenter the public because I had regained my identity and self-confidence, and I was renewed and determined to reclaim my work and lifestyle.

There would always be those who would never accept me or give me a chance because of my disfigurement. At the WBC, I had met others with similar physical challenges who had resumed their careers and relationships. I saw that it was possible to love; however, I firmly believed that only a man who had also endured the pain and angst of a burn could ever understand or accept me. As I closed my eyes, I wondered if Alex would call me as he had said he would.

The following day, at the airport, I confidently strode down the terminal concourse to the gate of my flight to Fort Lauderdale. I smiled as I boarded the crowded plane. I felt as if every eye was upon me as I walked down the aisle to my seat. I understood their curiosity because I'd experienced the same thing, wondering what had happened to the survivors I saw at the WBC, how they'd moved beyond their losses, and how they'd come to terms with their changed bodies and circumstances. The passengers on the plane were shocked by my appearance. They undoubtedly wondered what had happened to me, and how I lived with disfigurement. They probably thought, What if this happened to them?

The intrusive stares of strangers on the plane couldn't diminish the hope that I carried deep inside my heart, because I was a woman who owned her body and story. My scars were a sign of my strength and courage.

CHAPTER SIXTEEN

The First Time

There is a candle in your heart, ready to be kindled. There is a void in your soul, ready to be filled. You feel it, don't you?

Rumi

After the WBC

When Alex called, we talked for over two hours. I couldn't believe it. I rarely spoke to anyone on the phone for more than ten or fifteen minutes, unless it was Melissa. But as the days and weeks passed, Alex and I lingered on the phone for hours. Handwritten letters on yellow legal pad paper began to appear in the mailbox. The letters were progressive. He'd write in the morning, work for a while, and later write about another aspect of his life. I learned that he had filed for a divorce and had a daughter and a son. Night after night, we hated to say goodbye. Finally, after a month of talking by phone, we decided to meet, and since Alex lived in Colorado, he embraced the invitation to come to Florida in March.

I was excited about his visit but very nervous about the possibility of being intimate. I hadn't kissed a man in more than two years, much less made love! His burn injury had occurred many years before we met, and he'd grown comfortable with his appearance. I was still adjusting to my altered body and apprehensive that my extensive scarring might be too much for him. I had no idea what his body looked like because I'd only seen him dressed in slacks and a long-sleeved shirt.

Working around my ongoing surgery and therapy schedules, we decided on dates to get together for a long weekend. Alex wanted to go to Key West during his visit. I had been to Key West several times. Roger and I had attended a tennis camp there, so I was somewhat familiar with the colorful, bohemian southernmost point of the country.

Alex said he would reserve a car; upon his arrival, he rented a convertible and drove to the condo. Prompted by the gate attendant, I watched on the security system as Alex walked through the lobby to the security desk. Russell, my favorite guard, called to confirm that Alex could come up.

I opened the door and saw him striding down the hallway. "You made it!"

Grinning, he said, "It's wonderful to see you." Then, as he stepped inside the condo, he said, "Wow, what a stunning view you have."

We hugged.

"Here, come put your luggage down. Can I get you something to drink, a glass of wine or a beer?"

"A beer would be great."

"Would you like a glass or the bottle?"

"A glass would be perfect."

I poured myself a glass of wine and gave Alex a Tecate with lime. I rarely drank beer because I was allergic to the hops, but when I did, I preferred a citrus beer with a squeeze of lime. On a trip to Mexico, I first discovered Tecate. Typically, one glass of wine would not affect me, but at this moment, I hoped it might make me more relaxed.

Alex reached into his satchel and retrieved a small package. "I saw this and thought that you might like it." When I unwrapped and opened the box, I found a silver bracelet with a turquoise heart and toggle clasp. "It's beautiful. I love it." I clasped it around my wrist.

He reached back into his bag, retrieved a cassette tape, and handed it to me. "Let's listen to this. I made it for us. It has lots of songs that I think you'll like."

"Oh, it was so thoughtful of you to take the time to do this." I popped the tape into the player, dimmed the lights, and walked over to the sofa. I sat down beside him. The first track was Roberta Flack's song "The First Time Ever I Saw Your Face." He moved closer and placed his hand on my cheek. "I'll never forget the first time I saw your face." Then he kissed me. I didn't think about my scars, my limitations, or how I used to look. Instead, I felt the texture of his thick, short hair and the warmth of his body next to mine. We touched and kissed, enraptured by the moment and the romantic background music. The lyrics captured my every feeling and thought.

If Alex had been turned off by my scarred and disfigured body, I didn't know it.

The next day, we drove down to Key West in the convertible. During my recovery, I had fantasized about driving my convertible with the wind blowing on my face. I used to love driving and road trips. It was fun to once again be on an adventure in a convertible.

In Key West, we had fun exploring boutiques and cafés, and Alex was one of the few men I'd ever known who enjoyed shopping. We had a romantic dinner at sunset on Little Palm Island, which we reached by ferry. Our table was on the sand, next to the surf.

On the trip back to Fort Lauderdale, Alex wanted to stop

in the Everglades. I had no interest in going there but appreciated his desire to see it. Regrettably, we arrived near dusk, when the no-see-ums and every other bug and insect imaginable converged on the convertible. I'm arachnophobic and hate every creepy, crawly creature on earth. I couldn't wait to get out of the Everglades. When Alex said, "We'll have to get here earlier the next time," I knew there would not be a next time for me. I had no desire to return to the Everglades.

Later that evening, we went to Tom and Melissa's for dinner. Tom was a newly divorced father of two adorable little girls, Katherine, eight, and Machenta, six. Melissa had met him on a blind date instigated by one of my home-health aides. Recently, Melissa had moved in with Tom and the girls. It was fabulous to see her happy again after that awful Sunday morning more than a year ago when Ryan had unexpectedly appeared at the condo to break up with her. We were both stunned when the doorman called and said, "Good morning, Ms. Pell. There's a Ryan Russell here to see you. May I let him in?"

Melissa and I had exchanged looks of surprise and confusion. It was out of the ordinary for Ryan to be so spontaneous. "Oh my God, I hope he isn't here to give us bad news about Mom," I said. The doorbell rang. I opened the door and immediately sensed that something was wrong because of his nervous demeanor. "Come in. What a surprise to see you." Instead of his usual smile, he was tight lipped and tense.

"Hi, Charlene. I need to talk to Melissa privately for a few minutes." He looked around the condo. "Maybe outside, on the balcony?"

"Sure, I'll go into my room so you two can have some privacy."

They went outside, and I could tell by looking at their postures and the distance between them that something was wrong. Twenty minutes later, Ryan fled the condo without a word to me. Melissa was so devastated that she was hyperventilating just trying to speak. "He . . . just broke up with me. He's seeing someone else. He said he didn't plan to spend the rest of his life 'taking care' of you and that our lives would never be the same because of you. I tried to tell him how well you're doing and that someday you'll be independent again. I hate to even tell you this. I know how much it must hurt you."

I hugged her and tried to calm her, but she wept for hours. I, too, was stunned and hurt by Ryan's words, attitude, and actions. Throughout my six months at the rehab hospital, he had been supportive in every way. Almost weekly, he had sent exquisite tropical flower arrangements to brighten our days and visited as often as possible. Daily, he and Melissa had talked. She had thought that everything was fine between them and he understood that she needed to remain with me a while longer.

Melissa cried for months, until her anguish turned into anger. I had never seen her so broken before, even after the death of our father. Usually, Melissa exuded joy with her playful, youthful energy and enthusiasm. At that time, she was sad and easily cried all the time. It upset me to see her suffer, and I felt partially guilty for their breakup. She had spent months away from Ryan to take care of me. I knew that she had longed to be with both of us. I sensed how much she had missed him when they were apart, but she had never complained. On the days when she had returned home to Wilmington to visit Ryan, she had been jubilant, although she always cried whenever she had to leave me. His unexpected behavior blindsided us. We both felt betrayed and abandoned. Although I had reservations about Melissa moving in with Tom and the girls, I was relieved she had found a new love.

After leaving their house, I was tired, while Alex still had plenty of energy. He was used to walking and hiking and had more stamina than me. As we drove back to the condo, Alex said, "You know, it would be better if you didn't try to do so many things at one time"—not "Have you considered just focusing on one or two projects at a time, instead of six or seven?" His remark seared through me like a jolt of electricity. With a look of disdain, I quipped, "I don't need another man to tell me what to do." His comment disappointed me.

Most of the men in my life have been disappointing, beginning with my father. Mom said he was drunk on the day I was born; however, she loved him and stood by her man through all his escapades. My dad loved me mostly from afar, as he was a traveling salesman during my childhood. We were best buds until I began transforming from a child into a young girl. We fished on the Mississippi River and played shuffleboard on the bar of the local watering hole, and he taught me how to play gin rummy. Later, we played six to eight bingo cards every Wednesday night at the Elks Lodge. It was exhilarating to shout "bingo" and win money. Whatever game we played was for cash. But sadly, Dad's wagers on sports, racing, and cards got out of control, as did his drinking. It was upsetting to see him become intoxicated, even though he was a friendly, happy drunk when it happened. One night, as I walked behind him as he headed for our house's back door, he staggered and fell. Blood gushed from his forehead. I screamed for Mom as he began to get up. Dad was six feet two, while Mom was barely five feet tall.

Nevertheless, she helped to get Dad inside and attended to his injury. Despite my, Mom's, and Melissa's efforts to get Dad to stop drinking, he persisted until his death at the early age of forty-seven. He died of cirrhosis. For most of my young-adult life, I believed that my dad didn't love us enough to quit drinking. Later, I realized he was in the grip of a severe addiction driven by deep personal anguish relating to his childhood.

Despite my disappointment with Dad, he was fun, charming, charismatic, and intelligent, and I valued all those attributes. With hindsight, I realized that Roger had many of my dad's characteristics, except he rarely had drank too much and hadn't been into gambling.

My handsome, devoted first husband, my high school and college sweetheart, wasn't the man I had thought he was. My second husband had been an exceptional adulterer.

Since my injury, most of my doctors had been men, most of whom I liked and respected; however, they had been predicting what I could and couldn't do and what I needed to do to recover. All too often, they thought their way was the only way and were not open to alternative, proven treatments and procedures, such as peer support, acupuncture, and guided imagery.

Alex and I sat in silence for the remainder of the drive, until he parked the car. His eyes held a little less sparkle as we entered the door to the condo.

Like many couples in long-distance relationships, we were so excited to be together that we had overlooked some signs that we might need to be more compatible. I sensed that Alex was used to making all the decisions. I, too, was accustomed to controlling whatever I could and had been self-sufficient most of my adult life. I enjoyed the companionship of a man, but I didn't need a man in my life to be happy, fulfilled, and content.

Sadly, Alex and I had more fun on the phone than in person. Nevertheless, it was difficult for me to end the long-distance relationship, because I feared it might be my only chance for love, and Alex was a remarkable and talented man. He was missing three fingers on his left hand, yet he regularly ventured out into the wilderness to go canoeing with a buddy. In addition, he was an avid and excellent photographer; I marveled at how he manipulated a 35mm camera to capture breathtaking pictures of the places he visited. I, too, loved photography, especially shooting scenes of nature and close-ups of flowers and plants.

In one letter, he wrote, "What started out as a slow dance, a couple of brief conversations, a touch of your face has turned into what I hope can be a long-term commitment, if not a lifetime."

CHAPTER SEVENTEEN

What Shall We Call You Now?

*One knows what one has lost, but not what
one may find.*

George Sand

Returning to work after the crash

I arrived at DCOTA to meet with my boss, Joan, to discuss re-turning to work part time. As I entered her office, she greeted me with a huge smile and said, "It's wonderful to see you, dear. Come, sit down and let's talk about your return to work." Then she looked me in the eyes and said, "We need to figure out what we shall call you now."

My heart sank. I struggled to hold back my tears. As I felt my chest tighten, I tried to maintain my focus, despite the shock. So often, in the past, I had sat in this exact seat as a strong, vibrant, and competent vice president of communications. With everything else in my life stripped away, my career was the only visible thing left. I had been an integral part of the management team and had worked tirelessly to attain this executive level.

Joan and Mr. D. had visited me for months at the Burn Center and the rehab hospital. At one point, there had been a discussion about setting up a computer in my room at the rehab hospital so that I could do some work, but Dr. Sassoon advised that this would place too much stress on me and would interfere with my therapy and recovery.

"Since my accident, you and Mr. D. have constantly talked to me about returning to work. However, you never mentioned that I might be returning to a different position. What changed?"

"Dear, with your ongoing therapy and surgeries, you won't be able to manage all the responsibilities of VP. You know we value your work and opinion and want you to continue to work for DCOTA in a capacity that won't interfere with your recovery."

I felt nauseated just thinking about accepting a lesser position. Yet, through no fault of my own, I was weak, wounded, disfigured—and now displaced. I felt like the blood was draining out of my body, as if I were going to faint.

"We thought you might like to be director of special projects and oversee the Designer on Call program." I'd helped to create this program. The service offered consumers who might be reluctant to hire an interior designer the chance to meet for a one-hour complimentary consultation. We hoped the program would dispel myths about working with professional designers and create more business as well. "You could do this part time. What do you think?"

I didn't want this less significant role but realized I didn't have another choice. Realistically, I didn't have the strength or stamina to manage my former responsibilities as vice president, and ongoing surgeries and therapies would interfere for years. The additional stress would be damaging and delay my recovery. Still, I had been clinging to the hope that I at least might salvage my career, a massive part of my identity. Reluctantly, I said, "I'll give it a try." Disappointed, I got up from the chair and said goodbye.

I was upset and hurt. I felt like the only meaningful aspect remaining in my life had been seized without cause. And I knew Janet had replaced me.

In my absence, Janet Roda, a talented and experienced woman I had hired and mentored, had been named interim vice president of communications. I had fostered her career with DCOTA, and now she was doing my job.

Janet had visited me at the rehab hospital. I felt hostile toward her and resented that she was assuming my responsibilities, sitting in my chair at my desk, and doing everything I wished I could do. I told Janet how I felt, and I think she understood.

A week after meeting with Joan, I returned to DCOTA to begin my new job. Upon arrival, I discovered that I no longer had an office. Instead, my assigned desk was in a small cubicle outside my former office. I felt humiliated. Disappointment had always been the most painful emotion for me to contend with as a child and as an adult.

Shortly after my return to work, Joan asked me to help her recruit my replacement. I was a reluctant assistant. I didn't want to replace myself. However, it didn't take me long to realize that I didn't have the energy or stamina to work long hours, and stress exacerbated my pain and discomfort. Balancing work with ongoing rehabilitation and surgeries was all-consuming. Every eight weeks, I had another reconstructive surgery. Just as I would begin to become involved with a project, I would miss several weeks due to surgery and recovery. Simultaneously, I continued occupational, physical, and psychological therapy.

Several months after my return to work, I learned that

DCOTA was hosting a huge celebration to commemorate the organization's fifteenth anniversary. Dignitaries and guests from around the country had been invited to attend. The entire staff was busy working on the details of the party. A receiving line comprising the key employees and the owners would greet each guest.

It crushed me when Joan and Mr. Danto didn't invite me to be a part of the receiving line at the anniversary gala. I had contributed to DCOTA's success. I felt left out because of my disfigured appearance. All that I had invested in DCOTA was appreciated but seemed to have been forgotten. Or, at the very least, hidden. Once again, I was disappointed.

Nevertheless, Melissa, Tom, and I attended the formal affair. Melissa wore the sophisticated, ankle-length black skirt and sleeveless tuxedo-like top that I had worn at the opening gala of the *Women of Design* exhibition. The outfit reminded me of my contributions to DCOTA. It had taken more than a year to plan and coordinate that unprecedented exhibit showcasing the talent of female designers and architects. Ironically, in conjunction with this event, I had visited the Ryder Trauma Center at Jackson Memorial Hospital a few weeks before I became a patient. The exhibit opened on February 5 and ended on February 25, just four weeks before the crash.

Tom had rented a tuxedo to attend the gala. He and Melissa had never experienced such a prestigious event. Touring the exquisite, sophisticated showrooms of DCOTA gave them a glimpse into the glamorous industry of designer furnishings and a world of opulence they had only seen in the movies. White-gloved servers with silver trays circulated with flutes of champagne and canapés and scrumptious hors d'oeuvres. The scent of expensive, rare perfumes floated in the air. Ficus trees sat atop the Italian piazza marble of the atrium, which sparkled with tiny white lights. Designers, architects, builders, contractors, state and local officials, and clients nationwide gathered to celebrate DCOTA. It was a lavish affair that I would normally have planned and produced. But that time, I was a guest. For the first time since my injury, I wore a dress. It was a mandarin-style, floor-length, red satin dress with cap sleeves. Tubigrip covered my neck and arms, and custom-made nude gloves protected my hands. I wore the diamond bracelet that Mr. Danto had given me. The dress was also formfitting and uncomfortable, but I wanted to look my best for this special occasion. The skin on my arms was so sensitive that I couldn't tolerate anything touching my skin. Only cap sleeves or sleeveless tops were an option.

That evening, I walked more than I had since the accident. I was physically and emotionally exhausted when we returned to the condo. I was adjusting to my diminished stamina and physical challenges. Still, I felt a sense of personal and professional accomplishment by attending the anniversary celebration.

During the next few months, I felt unfulfilled by my work at DCOTA but did my best. My career seemed frivolous now, without depth and meaning. I was no longer interested in laboring for material things and status. Instead, I wanted to work to make a difference in the lives of other burn survivors who were adjusting to a disfigured appearance and the myriad of physical and emotional challenges.

At church, I participated in a project called the Spire Series. We had decided to book acclaimed recording artists for concerts in the sanctuary. Years before, when I worked for Citicorp, I had booked entertainers, so I was familiar with the process and enjoyed it. We engaged notable performers such as Judy Collins, Mark O'Connor, and Tuck and Patti for the Spire Series. As projected, we attracted crowds of newcomers to the church and the concerts. During intermission, I sold concessions to help the Phoenix Society. I continued to feel compelled to invest more time and effort to benefit this vital charity.

I was deeply honored that, after the ABA conference, Alan and Delwyn had asked me to succeed as director of the Phoenix Society. I traveled to their home in Pennsylvania to attend a camp for burned children and to work with Alan and Delwyn for a week. I needed to see firsthand what was required and assess what would be necessary to sustain the struggling charity. It was overwhelming. Essentially, the two of them did the work of five people, and it wasn't enough. They desperately needed financial and staffing help. Seeing all they accomplished was astounding, but the charity consumed their lives.

Due to my physical limitations and the ongoing surgeries and rehabilitation, I wasn't sure I wanted to switch places. I feared I couldn't give the organization a hundred percent of my time or energy. In addition, my experience told me that managing and growing the organization would be an all-consuming endeavor that would leave no time for a personal life. As much as I wanted to support the society's mission, I wasn't sure I wanted to embark on such a demanding project.

I returned to Florida confused and conflicted about what to do. I had exceptional health benefits and security at DCOTA, while everything about working for the Phoenix Society was a huge risk. I had regained the respect and acceptance of my colleagues and the design community as director of special projects, and I had years of reconstructive surgery ahead. I couldn't jeopardize my rehabilitation and recovery. Again, my health was interfering with my desire and dreams. A medical event in July 1997 determined my decision.

CHAPTER EIGHTEEN

Another Debilitating Setback

What does not kill me makes me stronger.

Friedrich Nietzsche

Three years after the crash

As I made my way out of a downward-facing-dog yoga position, I experienced unusual dizziness. It was the Thursday before the Fourth of July weekend. I thought the dizziness might subside after I ate something, but it didn't.

I'd been taking the antibiotic Keflex for three days to treat an infection in the middle finger of my left hand. Concerned, I called my orthopedic surgeon's office and told the assistant my symptoms. "Could this be an allergic reaction to the Keflex? I'm uncomfortable taking more of the pills until Dr. R. says it's okay."

"I'll let him know and have him call you, Ms. Pell," she said.

I was annoyed. This side effect was occurring at such an inopportune time. I had surgery scheduled for Tuesday, just a few days away. I needed to go to the grocery store and drugstore to pick up items in preparation. I postponed my errands and waited all afternoon for someone from my doctor's office to return my call. But no one did, and the dizziness continued.

Toward the end of the day, I called the doctor's office again. The phone on the other end rang, but no one answered.

I was furious. I'd spent my entire day expecting an answer that never came. It was almost time for my next dose of Keflex, and I wondered if I should risk taking more of it. What if I was having an allergic reaction? I didn't want to do anything that might worsen the vertigo or interfere with my upcoming surgery. Yet I had a severe infection in my finger and was afraid to stop the medication without my doctor's authorization.

The instructions on the Keflex label warned patients to finish all the medicine unless otherwise directed by their physician. Still, I was afraid to take the pill. Finally, after thinking about it for a few minutes, I reluctantly swallowed the capsule.

I began to shake uncontrollably within a few minutes of taking it, alone in my condo on the eighteenth floor. Terrified, I grabbed my wallet and the medicine bottle, fled my apartment, and hurried to the elevator. I pushed the down button, impatient for the doors to open. Once they did, I jumped on and rode the elevator to the first-floor lobby, rushing to the front desk to find a security guard or anyone to help me. I was relieved to see my favorite guard, Russell, standing behind the desk. He had always treated me with kindness and respect.

Leaning against the front desk, I used my diaphragm to draw air deep into my lungs to calm my nervous system and stop the shaking so that I could talk, but it didn't help.

"Russell, I think I'm having an allergic reaction to this medicine." I handed him the bottle of pills. "If I should lose consciousness, please show this medicine to the EMTs when they arrive. Hurry! Please call 911 for me."

"Okay, I'll call right away."

"I'm going to sit down on the sofa. The shaking is making

me feel off balance. And please call Melissa and tell her what's going on." I gave him the number.

"I'll call her now."

The hospital was only minutes away, and I was grateful to hear sirens and see the ambulance arrive under the canopy. In a moment, four male EMTs were inside assisting me. "Hi, ma'am, what is your name?" one of them asked.

Another said, "Ma'am, I'm going to put this cuff on your left arm to check your blood pressure."

"Did anything happen to upset you before this occurred?"

I explained that I thought I was reacting to the Keflex.

"Her vitals appear to point in the direction of an allergic reaction."

Another EMT attempted unsuccessfully to insert an IV into a vein above my left wrist. It seemed that the dense scar tissue hindered his efforts. He kept trying, frustrated but determined. Finally, I suggested he try the right arm. Among themselves, they agreed that they should get me to the ER right away.

Just as they helped me onto the gurney, Melissa and Tom rushed in. "What's wrong?" Melissa asked. I could see the look of concern and worry on her face, and I tried to quit shaking to tell her what had happened, as the EMTs wheeled me out to the ambulance. "We'll follow you to the hospital and meet you at the emergency room," she said. It was dusk as the ambulance sped out of the driveway and toward Federal Highway.

At Imperial Point Hospital everything blurred together as they took blood tests and monitored my vitals. They treated me with Benadryl intravenously, and once the shaking subsided, they released me. Safe at home, with Melissa in the next room, I crawled into bed and fell asleep.

But my ordeal wasn't over. In the morning, the symptoms recurred, so Melissa drove me to the emergency room, where the physicians monitored me until late afternoon. Once again, the shaking subsided. But unfortunately, the same thing happened again the next day. The ER doctor sent me home with prednisone, a strong steroid, to eliminate the shaking and flu-like symptoms and referred me to an allergy specialist. The aftereffects of that stressful weekend unfolded the same way a tiny crack in a windshield slowly spreads, eventually shattering the glass.

Because of my reaction to the Keflex and subsequent treatment, I had to postpone the surgical procedure that would have allowed me to turn my head to the left with greater ease. I was disappointed that I had to reschedule the operation, and I would have to repeat the preoperative blood test and a chest X-ray before I could have the surgery. I called my plastic surgeon, Dr. Michael Kelly, to tell him what had happened. I trusted this skilled, compassionate man.

"Don't worry about the operation. We'll reschedule it. More importantly, I want you to have an allergy test to see if you are also allergic to penicillin. Then we'll call you with a new date for the operation. In the meantime, let me know about the allergy-test results."

During the next two weeks, I gradually regained my strength and stamina. I resumed a few typical activities, such as preparing food, doing laundry, and driving to and from the nearby grocery store. Unfortunately, I couldn't return to work at DCOTA yet, so I passed the time with books and organizing a fundraising project for the Phoenix Society. After two more weeks, I was eager to return to work and my normal activities. However, I dreaded the thought of undergoing an allergy test. I was afraid I might have another reaction, with symptoms worse than those I had just experienced. Still, Dr. Kelly and my general practitioner, Dr. O'Dell, insisted that I have the test.

With trepidation, I drove to the clinic to have the allergy test. The petite female doctor greeted me in a white lab coat that covered her blouse and skirt. She examined my abdomen to find a reliable "test site" to administer the trial. Her layered hair brushed against my face, and I detected a light, exotic fragrance as she bent over to prick the skin. The pale skin on my abdomen rose and turned pink, like a mosquito bite. "Perfect, I think we have a reliable site, so let's begin the test," she said. She instructed the nurse to inject minute doses of cephalosporin and penicillin into my bloodstream.

Within a few minutes, I said, "I feel like my legs are swelling." Because of the second- and third-degree burns to my legs, the skin was now thin, like Saran Wrap, but tight, like snakeskin, from my ankles to the tops of my thighs, so the nurse couldn't detect any swelling.

But I could feel it. "Please ask the doctor to look at my ankles and legs before you continue."

She called for the doctor, who returned, pressed her fingers firmly on my ankles, and said, "I don't see any significant swelling. You're fine. I think you're having a panic attack."

I was swelling. I could feel pressure inflating like a balloon inside my rubbery skin. The determined allergy specialist insisted that I was "only" experiencing a panic attack and that we should complete the test. She seemed more concerned about being correct than about my well-being. I didn't want to continue the test. Still, I knew it was imperative for determining if I was allergic to the antibiotics, so I endured the temporary distress. Progressively, I felt worse.

I completed the test and left the specialist's office concerned and upset. Unfortunately, she had not been receptive to my feelings or the possibility that my responses might not have manifested according to normal protocol because of my burns.

Hungry, I drove around the block to a shopping mall to eat lunch. As I walked through the Lord & Taylor department store, I glanced at myself in a mirror in the cosmetics area—I was white as snow. I hadn't eaten anything since breakfast, so

I attributed my lightheadedness to hypoglycemia. I walked to the food court to one of my favorite Greek restaurants and was standing at the counter about to order spanakopita and a Greek salad when I began to shake uncontrollably and felt faint. Scared, I hurried to my car, returned to the doctor's office, and rushed inside.

I told the receptionist, "Something's wrong. I shouldn't be shaking like this. I feel like my tongue is swelling."

"Call the doctor on her cell and ask her what she wants us to do," the nurse said to the receptionist.

I overheard the nurse's remarks to the doctor, and then the nurse said, "Call for the paramedics, just to be safe."

Within minutes, the paramedics arrived and rushed into the clinic lobby with a stretcher. As they wheeled me out to the ambulance, I saw the look of panic on the faces of patients waiting for treatment. The medics whisked me off to the closest hospital, where I remained for ten hours while being treated for anaphylactic shock, a severe and sometimes fatal systemic reaction.

I asked one of the female EMTs, "Could you please call my sister and tell her where I am and what has happened? I know that she will be worried about me."

Instead, she handed me the phone and smiled. "Here, you call her." Her gesture reassured me that I was going to be okay. Relieved, I dialed Melissa's number and explained what had happened. As always, she rushed to my side and accompanied me throughout the frightening ordeal. I was discharged from the ER near midnight. Melissa drove me home. I was exhausted and angry.

During the next two weeks, I experienced debilitating symptoms of muscle weakness, headaches, swelling, fainting, and aches and pains in all my muscles and joints. Dr. O'Dell referred me to a rheumatologist, who discovered that I had an elevated erythrocyte sedimentation (SED) rate, a blood test result that indicates inflammatory activity in the body, which could cause the bizarre, debilitating symptoms. Many illnesses are related to high SED rates, which track the body's inflammation.

After the anaphylactic shock reaction, every day was worse than the day that preceded it. My condition rapidly deteriorated, so I had to ask my mom to return to Florida to live with me. I was too weak to prepare meals or do ordinary tasks like laundry or grocery shopping. I was distraught and so discouraged—after all that I had endured to recover my life and work, my progress was interrupted. I blamed the allergy specialist for my setback. She accepted no responsibility for my prolonged disability. She insisted that despite the diagnosis of a "mild anaphylactic reaction," I didn't have an adverse reaction to the test. She could simply place my patient file in a drawer and forget about me. Meanwhile, I had to live with unbearable symptoms and treatment.

I recalled reading a prayer of St. Francis de Sales that says, "He will either shield you from suffering, or give you unfailing strength to bear it." Daily, I prayed, *God, please heal my body and stop the miserable symptoms. Please give me strength and patience to endure. Guide me to resources and people that might provide some relief.* It was challenging to hold on to hope and remain optimistic while feeling like a prisoner of my body and the health care system.

One night in August, as I lay in bed restless and unable to sleep, I was shocked to see a news clip on television announcing that Princess Diana was clinging to life in a French hospital. Photos of the crushed black limo that she and Dodi al-Fayed had been traveling in jarred my very being. I couldn't believe my eyes or ears. Throughout that night, I followed every report until I heard the devastating words: "Princess Diana has died at a Paris hospital." I was overcome with grief, as if one of my closest friends had died. Sadness suffused me like toxic fumes from an exhaust pipe. My sorrow compounded my health struggles and eroded my optimism. How could such an important, vital woman like Princess Diana die? Her death shook the core of my soul. For weeks, I tearfully mourned for this remarkable young woman. Diana was like an elegant, ethereal water lily floating atop the murky waters of a world filled with sin and injustice.

For the first time, I understood the sadness and grief that my family and friends must have experienced after witnessing my catastrophic injury, the ensuing disfigurement, and the ongoing pain and suffering required to repair my damaged body. I imagined they also longed for the attractive, vibrant woman I was before the burn injury. They mourned for the other Charlene but were thrilled that I remained alive, even in my damaged condition.

Princess Diana's untimely death made me question my existence. I wondered if I, too, might die an unfinished life.

CHAPTER NINETEEN

Farewell, Dear Hal

*The best and most beautiful things in the
world cannot be seen nor even touched, but
just felt in the heart.*

Anne Sullivan

Three years after the crash

One cold, starlit evening during Christmastime in 1995, Mom, Hal, Melissa, and I had visited Hal's son CH and his wife, Mia, in their new home in Pleasant Garden. We climbed out of the car and walked up the steps to the front door of a traditional, two-story brick house. Several dogs began to bark. Before we could ring the doorbell, a tall, slender man with salt-and-pepper hair and dark-rimmed glasses opened the door and said, "Hey, good evening, come inside out of the cold. We've been expecting you."

A tiny, barking, hyperactive, black-and-tan miniature pinscher named Mattie led us into the living room. CH's wife, Mia, appeared. She had a cheerful face and rosy cheeks sprinkled with freckles and curly, light, reddish-blonde hair. She wore an oversized gray sweatshirt, sweatpants, socks, and clogs.

Candlesticks glowing in all the windows were the only sign of Christmas. Their home felt cold and devoid of love and happiness. There were no photographs of family and friends. Instead, bookcases were stuffed with history books, especially about the Civil War.

CH noticed me looking at the books and commented, "Mia is quite a history buff."

A gray parrot perched in a cage situated adjacent to the fireplace.

Melissa and I liked birds and previously had owned cockatiels, so we wandered over to talk to the parrot. CH walked over to the cage, stuck his arm in, and brought the bird out so that we could get a better look at him. "This is Henry. Look out for your earrings; he likes to try to take them out. He's been known to draw blood!"

"Yikes," I said. We moved away from Henry and returned to our seats.

Henry took off and landed on top of a drapery rod. We chatted about plans for the rest of the holiday weekend, and Mom said, "We'd love to have you two join us for Christmas dinner."

CH said, "Oh, thank you so much, but we'll be spending the day with Mia's family, but please save us some of your awesome pound cake!"

Hal asked Mia, "Do you have any dates at churches nearby for the Lottie Moon Christmas offerings?"

"Who is Lottie Moon?" I asked.

Mia said, "She was a missionary to China who urged Southern Baptists to start an annual offering to support international missions. I reenact her life story at churches from Thanksgiving to Christmas."

"Wow, how did you get involved in that?" I asked.

"Someone in the Woman's Missionary Union asked me to tell the story of Lottie Moon."

CH said, "She created a monologue to tell the story, and word spread from one church to another. So now we're traveling all over North Carolina and South Carolina every weekend so that she can perform. I manage the setup and sound."

I asked Mom, "Have you ever been to one of the performances?"

"No, but we'll have to do that next year. Right now, we'd better get going. I know everyone is getting hungry."

We bundled up to go outside into the frigid air to return to Mom's cozy home and a crackling fireplace. I had become more comfortable with fireplaces by this point.

Several months later, I saw CH again. But until then, I hadn't known how unhappy he was that winter evening when we had first met.

Mia left CH six months after that Christmas, and I only saw him once before the following Christmas in 1996. Sitting around Mom's dining room table, he told me about his strained relationship and separation. He explained that he had lost his job of seventeen years just two weeks after they had bought the new home. The move to the new, bigger home had been an attempt to make Mia happy. As CH's life was crumbling, Hal was fighting for his life. Skin cancer had invaded his lymph nodes and lungs.

It was agonizing for Mom, Melissa, and me to witness Hal's decline. I loved Hal. He had been a devoted, loving caregiver to me during my stay at the rehab hospital. He was gentle and patient and demonstrated love and concern for all of us. Throughout my rehabilitation, he'd traveled back and forth between North Carolina and Florida to help Mom and me. While Mom stayed with me in Florida, Hal had managed everything around Mom's house, while continuing his treatments and procedures. Mom was always calmer and happier whenever

Hal was nearby. I marveled as he gallantly attempted to participate in all the annual Christmas festivities, despite his fatigue and pain.

When Melissa and I left Hal and Mom at the airport that Christmas in 1996, I fought back the rush of tears. I wanted to put time on pause. I couldn't bear to think about the devastating impact that Hal's death would have on Mom and CH. It seemed so unfair that this magnificent man was dying. Tears rolled down my face as I turned one more time to wave goodbye to Hal, fearing I'd never see him alive again.

A few months later, Melissa and I planned a trip back to Greensboro to be with Hal for his April 12 birthday. Each day, he became weaker and thinner, and it was uncertain whether he would live to reach his birthday. Mom, CH, and his brother, James, had planned a celebration for the eleventh. In Florida, Melissa and I were busy preparing our things to travel to Greensboro when the phone rang.

"Hello, this is CH. I wanted to let you know before you leave that Dad died this morning."

"I'm so sorry that we didn't make it in time to say goodbye," I said, tears choking off that final word. "We should have changed our plans. Arrived earlier. I'm sorry that we weren't there."

"It's okay, Dad knew how much you both loved him. He died peacefully here with all of us. I'm planning to meet you girls at the airport. I'll see you at the baggage claim, okay?"

"Are you sure that you feel like picking us up? We can take the shuttle."

"I want to meet you. I'll see you in a few hours. Have a safe flight."

"May I speak to Mom for a minute? How is she?" I sank into a dining room chair. Nothing I could say would ease the devastating heartbreak she felt. I hated to see her cry or to be sad. I wanted to take her pain away.

"Under the circumstances, she is holding up well. I think she's trying to be strong for us."

"That sounds like our 'Steel Magnolia.'" I'd bestowed this nickname of endearment on Mom after seeing the movie *Steel Magnolias*.

"Hi, sweetie," she said as her voice quavered. "He's gone. We were by his side when he died. That's what he wanted . . . you girls finish getting ready, so you won't miss your flight. Have a safe trip and we'll see you in a few hours. It's going to be a very long day. I love you."

"We love you and we'll see you this afternoon."

We wiped away our tears and rushed to gather our belongings before we drove to the airport to catch our flight. Consumed with thoughts about Mom, CH, and James, I wasn't as sensitive to the stares of bystanders as we walked through the airport and cleared security to board our plane. During the flight, we fondly remembered the times spent with Hal. He and Mom had been inseparable, always smiling, laughing, and exchanging endearing glances. Whenever Mom was with him, she had been radiant and happy, like a teenager in love for the first time. Now, he was gone forever.

It seemed unbelievable that Mom had lost another man in her life. Wasn't it enough that our father had died so young, and our stepfather had died thirteen years after they'd married? Mom had devoted her life to caring for these men during their prolonged, debilitating illnesses.

My thoughts returned to the present as the plane slowed and then taxied to the gate. We deplaned and walked down the corridor toward the baggage claim area. CH spotted us and said, "Welcome home, it's wonderful to see you girls. Let me carry that heavy bag. Have you girls eaten lunch?"

"We're fine; we can make a sandwich when we get to Mom's." I dreaded entering Mom's house, imagining I would find a houseful of family and friends, somber and whispering, like the day of my dad's funeral. I wasn't emotionally or physically prepared to manage more grief, heartache, and disappointment.

Upon arrival, we found James sequestered in the front bedroom, writing a poignant tribute to Hal. Mom sobbed when she saw us. We hugged her and told her that we would get through this together.

There would be a visitation that evening at the funeral home. Unlike many friends and family members of departed loved ones, I disliked visitations. It seemed sacrilegious to me for guests to be so nonchalant in the presence of a dead person, talking and laughing in line as they waited for their turn to express their sympathy to the family. Plus, the family had to endure the draining emotional stress twice in less than twenty-four hours. Nevertheless, I told myself I could get through the visitation, and wanted to comfort Mom and CH.

The day of the funeral, as we were about to leave Mom's house to attend the memorial service, I looked at CH and said, "I wish that I could place a beautiful woman by your side to be with you throughout this unbearable day, but I'll have to do."

He smiled, and we walked outside and climbed into the black limousine. The fifteen-mile ride to the church was silent and seemed to take forever. Finally, we arrived in Summerfield at Center United Methodist Church, where Mom had been a member much of her life. Hal used to attend church there with her. Side by side, CH and I walked down the aisle to the second row from the front of the sanctuary, reserved for family. Melissa stayed next to Mom.

Throughout the touching tribute, CH held my hand and squeezed it so tight it hurt. I saw that he was fighting to hold back tears, as I was. Reverend Miller and Hal had been friends, so he shared personal memories of conversations and recounted experiences that they had enjoyed together. I wished that none of us were there and that Hal wasn't dead.

As I gazed at the spray of yellow roses caressing Hal's

casket, I remembered the first time that I met him at Mom's house, before my injury. He gave me a lovely photo of one of his orchids and asked me to wear it like a corsage. I felt it was a weird request, so I didn't wear it. Mom, of course, proudly pinned the photo to her blouse. Mom always thought of others before herself. I wished that I had given him that one sweet moment. On that sad spring day, Hal couldn't see or smell the fragrance of the hundreds of exquisite flowers dedicated to his life.

As I listened to the words spoken at the graveside, I remembered how he had loved orchids and yellow roses, his love for others, and his patience, understanding, nurturing, caring, and gentle ways. I will never forget his spirit of playfulness and humor, his love of puzzles and challenges, and his deep love for CH, James, Mom, Melissa, and me. Somehow, we endured the graveside service. Afterward, as a friend snapped a photo of us, CH placed his arm around my waist.

We solemnly returned home with so much sadness in our hearts, salty tears rolling down our cheeks and pooling in our mouths. The only source of any comfort was that we had each other and that, for the ride back to Mom's home, we were protected from the harsh reality that life never stops for the brokenhearted families and friends left behind to mourn the loss of a loved one. In the days, weeks, months, and years to come, the public wouldn't recognize or care about the loss and suffering we continued to feel. Only I had exterior scars to alert others that something horrible had happened in my life. CH, James, Mom, Melissa, and millions of other people looked "normal," so their suffering would go unnoticed except by friends and other family members aware of their loss.

The family car pulled into the driveway next to Mom's small yard, which was shaded by two white dogwood trees. We climbed out of the car and went inside. The house felt empty, like a theater after the audience has left. The sweet fragrance of stargazer lilies lingered in the living room. Pictures of Hal were on the mantle, television, end tables, and everywhere I looked. I was overwhelmed and felt an urge to escape the house and the sorrow inside.

I looked at CH and said, "Let's go for a walk. It's so beautiful outside."

"Sure, that sounds good. Let me take off this tie and jacket. I'll be out in a minute."

Mom was sitting in the recliner. I asked her, "Do you want to go with us?"

"No, you two go ahead. I'll be fine."

We ventured out together into the neighborhood where I had grown up. The azaleas were bountiful with white and fuchsia blossoms, the grass was a rich green, and the air was still cool enough for me to be comfortable. Pink and white dogwoods were abundant with blooms. Towering walnut, oak, maple, and evergreen trees lined the street. It felt refreshing and uplifting to be surrounded by the resplendence of nature, proof of life. After about thirty minutes, we turned a corner and headed back toward Mom's house when CH stopped beneath a crooked pink dogwood tree. He reached over, placed his hands above my wrists, and said, "I want to talk to you about something you said this morning that troubled me."

Mystified by what he meant, I waited for him to continue. "Remember when you said that you wished that you could place a pretty woman by my side to accompany me today?" It felt like one of those moments in the movies when the guy would have pulled the girl close and kissed her. CH said, "You have a beauty that transcends anything physical."

I melted like ice cream on a sweltering summer day. *He sees through the scars. He understands who I am, trapped in this altered body.*

After we went back inside the house, CH rubbed his temples and squinted his eyes. I asked, "Do you have a headache?"

"Yes, I've had one most of the day."

"Have you taken something for it?"

"Yes, but it's not working too well."

"Why don't you lie down on the sofa and relax. I'll massage your temples with this herbal cream with eucalyptus, called Peace of Mind. It has a fresh, invigorating scent. Here, smell. What do you think?"

"Let's give it a try." He stretched out on Mom's gold, upholstered sofa. His feet dangled off the end. I gently stroked his forehead, feeling the arched shape of his brow and gazing at his high, well-defined cheekbones and his chiseled lips and nose. His skin was smooth, soft, and supple.

Mom was resting in her swan mahogany rocking chair opposite the sofa. As I examined CH lying there, I noticed his broad shoulders, the rise and fall of his chest, his strong, wide neck, and his hips, legs, and stockinged feet. He looked sorrowful but handsome, dressed in dark-blue pinstripe pants and a starched white dress shirt.

I found myself wishing that Mom wasn't sitting opposite us. As I massaged CH's temple, neck, and head and saw how my body was helping his relax, I felt attracted to him as a lover. Was it possible that he could be more than a friend?

CHAPTER TWENTY

A Painful Parting

*Why does it take a minute to say hello and
forever to say goodbye?*

Author unknown

Three years after the crash

When I continued seeing Alex after his visit following the
WBC, I often talked to Dr. Mic about the relationship. He
said I was sabotaging it, especially after I told Dr. Mic about a
ten-day trip out west with Alex. During the trip, part business
and part pleasure, we visited spiritual, breathtaking places
like Sedona, the Grand Canyon, Monument Valley, Antelope
Canyon, and the Colorado River. Yet I felt less in love with him
as each day passed. One evening in Sedona, I was especially
looking forward to going to a romantic dinner at a fabulous
restaurant by a mountain stream. Alex returned from a trade
show tired and said he was going to take a nap.

"Shall I wake you in an hour or so?"

"No, I'll get up."

While he slept, I ventured outdoors and sat by a tranquil stream as I perused travel magazines about the area. An hour and a half later, I returned to the room and found him still sleeping. Our dinner reservation was in thirty minutes. I wanted to go to the dinner we had planned, but I wasn't sure if I should wake him. As I sat and watched him sleep, I was overcome with disappointment. I decided not to disturb him. Another hour and a half later, when he woke up, I was angry. However, he was not overly concerned.

When I told Dr. Mic about this experience, he said, "Why didn't you wake Alex? This is an example of what I meant when I said you appear to be sabotaging the relationship."

Instead, I used the incident to fuel my discontent with Alex.

Later, in a letter, Alex explained that business had been off, and he had been hesitant about going to such an expensive restaurant and adding to his debt. Instead, he wanted to enjoy the lovely B and B where we had stayed—the B and B that didn't serve dinner, and the B and B where he had primarily slept. His letter also said that he didn't value exceptional dining experiences as much as I seemed to.

On our first rendezvous, in Key West, I had booked a modest hotel in a convenient location. Upon our arrival, I was a little disappointed, but the proximity to shops and restaurants compensated for the lack of amenities. Alex remarked that he wished we had reserved a higher-end hotel on the ocean. Unfortunately, he never mentioned this during our evening phone calls. I, too, would have preferred something that felt special.

I wished he had talked to me directly about money issues and his feelings about dining at gourmet restaurants. I've always appreciated exceptional food and have had the privilege of eating at outstanding restaurants. He knew that I loved to cook and experiment with new recipes. He must have seen copies of *Food & Wine, Southern Living,* and *bon appétit* around the condo. Discovering new foods and wines, appreciating methods of presentation, and experiencing the ambiance of unique restaurants were some of my favorite things. Had he told me what was going on and shared his genuine feelings, we could have avoided the disappointing evening in Sedona.

This incident was one of several that marked the sad realization that there would not be a "happily ever after" in our future. We were entitled to our own perspectives about how our money and time should be spent. Alex was happiest on an adventure in the wild; I delighted in the comfort of a lovely environment with picturesque gardens, art, and fine food. I loved the theater and the symphony. Earlier in my career, I had lived and worked in Manhattan and had never felt more alive. Alex was strong and rugged; I was frail and physically vulnerable. Alex also had two adult children. After the disappointing experience with Roger's children, I was reluctant to get involved in another family's ordeals. Still, I loved so many things about Alex, but our lifestyles were out of sync. I felt guilty that I could no longer return his love. *Should I settle and just be thankful that he loves me?* I had wanted this relationship to work out, but I couldn't deny my deepest feelings.

On the last evening of our trip out west, my voice had cracked as I said, "It breaks my heart to tell you that I just don't think we have a future together." Overcome with emotion, my eyes were bloodshot from crying, my cheeks were stained with tears, and I had gone through a box of Kleenex wiping my runny, red nose. Alex hugged me. I was exhausted and, like Alex, very disappointed.

I fought back the tears throughout the flight home, feeling like I'd lost my best friend. I told myself this wasn't the first time a relationship hadn't worked out. Still, it seemed monumental in view of my changed circumstances and altered appearance. Yet I knew I would rather be lonely without a man than be lonely and unhappy with one.

I started to believe that despite my disfigurement, perhaps a remarkable man who was not necessarily a burn survivor or a man with physical challenges could love me. Crossing this mental threshold opened my mind to more possibilities. Alex had given me a priceless, timeless gift—my womanhood. For that, I was eternally grateful.

CHAPTER TWENTY-ONE

Baptists Don't Dance

And when you get the choice to sit it out or dance, I hope you dance.

Lee Ann Womack

Almost four years after the crash

Melissa's face beamed as she pranced into my bedroom and held out her left hand for me to see a sparkling diamond engagement ring. "Look, can you believe it? I'm finally going to get married. Isn't the ring beautiful? It's exactly what I wanted."

I sat up in bed, stunned that she had answered yes to the proposal. "The ring is exquisite, but are you sure you're not rushing into this?"

I hated to spoil her jubilation, but I didn't want to see her make a severe mistake. Tom was a sharp young man of modest means. Melissa had become accustomed to a luxurious lifestyle with her former companion of nine years, Ryan.

By marrying Tom, Melissa would instantly become a wife and a stepmother. Given her comfortable and carefree former lifestyle with Ryan, I worried that this might be too severe an adjustment all at once, but she was in love and excited about planning the wedding.

I wanted to contribute everything possible to make it the day of her dreams. I was grateful for this chance to express my gratitude to her. She had given up so much for me.

I was especially looking forward to shopping for a wedding gown together. But while Melissa was trying on dresses at a shop on Las Olas Boulevard, I turned white as a sheet and collapsed.

"Tom and I have been talking, and we think we should postpone the wedding until you feel better," she said after the incident.

"Regrettably, no one seems to be able to tell me when or if I will ever feel better. I don't want you to postpone the wedding. I'll just do the best that I can to participate in the festivities."

I remained optimistic and worked diligently to recover my strength and health. I researched and read every book I could find about healing and the connection between mind, body, and spirit. I was especially encouraged by my findings in Dr. Andrew Weil's book *Spontaneous Healing.* I discovered that eliminating all dairy products, eating less meat, adding fresh sources of omega-3 fatty acids, and eliminating all polyunsaturated and partially saturated fats from my diet might rid or ease arthritis aches and pains. I hadn't eaten red meat for seventeen years, so that was on my side. I'd never really liked meat and believed that it contributed to cancer.

I learned that swimming, practicing relaxing breathing, and psychotherapy might bring some relief. I discovered guided imagery and read case studies of patients who had improved with integrative medicine when conventional medicine didn't work.

I found proof that hope, faith, laughter, and the will to live are biochemical factors that can help to combat serious illnesses, in Norman Cousins's book *Head First: The Biology of Hope and the Healing Power of the Human Spirit.* Endocrinologist Deepak Chopra offered a new understanding of health, illness, and the healing power of the mind in his book *Creating Health.*

Dissatisfied with the dismal results of treatments prescribed by my local physicians, I consulted experts at the Mayo Clinic. I scheduled appointments with a vascular specialist, a neurologist, an endocrinologist, and an allergy specialist. Melissa and I drove six hours to Jacksonville, Florida, to meet with the specialists.

I was so impressed by this excellent clinic. My appointments were conveniently scheduled one after another in the same building. By the time I met each new physician, he had already reviewed the comments of the previous physician. I had never experienced such well-organized, interactive, and orchestrated health care.

After three days of extensive examinations, consultations with specialists, lab work, and tests, the specialists told me that I was in menopause, suffering from neuropathic pain, and that my lymphatic system was not functioning optimally.

The vascular specialist advised that I should avoid salt and resume wearing custom pressurized stockings to facilitate the flow of lymphatic fluid in my body. He gave me a list of things to do to prevent swelling in my extremities.

The neurologist explained that the stinging, burning, creepy-crawly feelings that radiated just below the surface of the thin skin on my arms and legs were caused by a condition called paresthesia. The tormenting sensations might be alleviated with antidepressants. There was some research to substantiate this assertion.

I dreaded the thought of taking a new medication. Because of the anaphylactic reaction, I had become more terrified of swallowing a pill that I had never taken than of boarding an airplane. I didn't want to depend on medicine that might have side effects worse than the current symptoms I was experiencing. Yet I was desperate for some relief. Battling the crippling symptoms of these conditions was wearing me down, physically and emotionally. I didn't like the sensation of hopelessness.

The endocrinologist recommended that I start hormone-replacement therapy. The first day of treatment, I had a negative reaction to the medicine during our drive home to Fort Lauderdale. My hope plummeted. I was disappointed but reassured that there was a physiological basis for my painful, bizarre, and life-interrupting symptoms.

Throughout this exasperating time, CH sent funny and touching cards and called more frequently. I wished we lived closer to one another, as almost a thousand miles separated us. He never mentioned any close friends, and I suspected that he was lonely. I encouraged him to participate in singles groups so that he could meet attractive, intelligent, available women. He joined a singles group at church that met for social outings.

During a conversation with my mom, she said, "CH has started dating a woman with a son." I experienced a sinking feeling in my stomach and was surprised by my reaction.

"Really? That's interesting. He hasn't mentioned that to me." It seemed natural that he'd bring up this woman during our conversations, since I'd been instrumental in coaching him on how to resume a dating life. But then I was perplexed about why it mattered to me. He continued to call, despite his newfound romance.

One night when we talked, he said, "I'm taking some shag lessons. I'm not very good at it, but I'm having fun. Growing up in such a strict Baptist home, we never got to listen to popular music or go to dances. Baptists don't dance. I don't have much rhythm, but I enjoy the lessons." He was speaking faster than usual, and I detected his excitement. I was happy to hear that he was doing something to socialize with other people.

When CH called, we often talked about Melissa and Tom's November wedding. CH planned to attend. The ceremony would be at the chapel where we were members, First Presbyterian Church of Pompano Beach. Melissa dreamed of hosting the reception on a yacht. Mom and I hoped to combine our resources to make that dream come true.

During the summer, Melissa and I completed arrangements for the wedding and reception. From songs to shoes, cake to the ceremony, veils to vows, flowers to formals, tuxedos to tables, we worked to create her dream wedding.

In private, I doubled down on efforts to improve my health, as I did not want to ruin Melissa's wedding by passing out while walking down the aisle. I practiced yoga daily, ate organic food, juiced carrots, and continued occupational, physical, and psychotherapy. Day by day, I grew stronger. CH called more often. I was relieved that he was coming to Florida for the wedding and looked forward to spending several days with him. I knew that I could rely on him to assist with everything. I had discovered that CH was competent and highly proficient at many things. I admired and appreciated these traits.

Summer melted into fall. Before we knew it, the weekend of the wedding had arrived. Tom had arranged for an oceanfront room for CH at the Deerfield Beach Embassy Suites, a tropical resort where Tom worked as chief engineer.

I met CH at the airport and drove him to the hotel. Later, he accompanied me to the rehearsal and to San Angel for dinner. The intimate, gourmet, southwestern restaurant had become a favorite place for Melissa and me to celebrate. CH looked handsome in his dark-blue pinstripe suit, starched white shirt, silk tie, and spit-shined black loafers. I loved his salt-and-pepper hair. There was a calmness about him that put me at ease. He sat next to me during dinner at San Angel. He was thoughtful and attentive throughout the evening. Melissa smiled as she and Tom relished their special occasion, surrounded by loved ones. It was renewing to see her and Mom so happy after all the angst that she, Mom, and I had endured.

After dinner, CH drove me home and dropped me off at the condo. "I had a great time," he said. "Try to get some rest. It's going to be a long day tomorrow. And thanks for trusting me with your car. I'll be over at ten thirty in the morning."

Like Cinderella, I didn't want this magical evening to end, but I was tired, so I said good night and walked inside.

On Saturday morning, CH arrived and loaded the trunk with the box holding the place cards, guest registration book, and gifts for Tom's girls. I was dressed in the royal-blue dress Melissa had chosen for me, which had a long satin skirt and bodice and glimmering rhinestone buttons. Under the vest-like top, I wore a champagne-colored lace blouse with cap sleeves. For weeks, I had searched for just the right, soft, comfortable blouse to cover the cord-like scars above my breasts. I couldn't tolerate any blouses with sleeves, seams, or irritating fabric that touched the skin on my burned arms. Therefore, it was always challenging to find comfortable, fashionable clothing. For the first time since my injury, I wore one-inch pumps. I felt awkward and a little off balance, but feminine. Inside the car, CH said, "You look pretty."

"I actually feel pretty today," I said as I smiled in appreciation. Only Melissa had ever commented that I looked pretty.

CH appeared even more attractive than the evening before, dressed in a tailored, fitted black suit, white dress shirt, and perfectly knotted silk tie. I felt drawn to him as we drove to the chapel.

"I still can't believe that Melissa is actually getting married," I said. "I wish she would wait for a while, but she says that this is what she wants."

"You're very protective of her, aren't you?"

"I know. Sometimes I feel more like a mother than a sister. I just want the best for her."

"Looks like we're here," CH said as we pulled into the chapel's parking lot.

We climbed out of the car and walked into the chapel. Linda, Mom's devoted niece, greeted us. She had everything under control. She and her husband, Bobby, had driven from North Carolina so that she could direct the wedding. The flowers were in place, as well as the candles, programs, guest book, and aisle runner.

A few guests arrived, and CH greeted them in the sanctuary. At the same time, I walked to the private room reserved for the wedding party, where Mom was clasping her pearls around Melissa's neck in honor of the tradition of wearing "something old." The "something new" was a lacy garter bound around her muscular thigh.

"Now, Machenta and Katherine, remember to look at the guests and smile as you sprinkle the rose petals on the white runner, okay? Aunt Linda will tell you when to walk down the aisle, just like we practiced last night," I reminded the girls. They were shy and nervous about their role. Their ankle-length dresses were made of the same royal-blue satin as mine but had empire waists and satin ribbon ties. Their cream-colored, ruffled socks showed when they walked. This was the first time that Machenta had been in a wedding and the second time for Katherine. They giggled with excitement. I brushed their shiny, thick, dark-brown hair and then stooped over and handed each one of them a little silver-wrapped gift.

"What's inside, Aunt Buddy?" Katherine asked as she began to tear open the package. Since my injury, Melissa always called me "Buddy." The girls knew me as "Aunt Buddy."

"It's something special for you to wear today and to keep forever."

"Look, Katherine, it's a pearl necklace! Thanks, Aunt Buddy," Machenta said.

"Here, let me clasp them for you," Mom said. "Oh, they look perfect, girls. You both look precious."

The pianist began to play the prelude selections. I turned to Melissa and hugged her. "More than anything in the world, I pray that you will be happy and that you two will share a lifetime of love. You deserve the best, my dear sister. I'll see you at the altar."

"Thank you for everything you've done to make this day so perfect. You're the best sister in the world. I love you," Melissa said.

Tears welled in my eyes, and I struggled to prevent them from gushing down my face and onto my top. I didn't have time to repair my makeup; I had to stop crying.

My mom told me that when I was upset as a little girl, I used to say, "I'll cry tomorrow." I needed that determination today.

Every pew was filled when I returned to the chapel and strode down the aisle. When I looked back at Melissa, I wished that our father was alive to escort her down the aisle. Unfortunately, he'd died when she was only sixteen.

Melissa is a lot like our dad, gregarious and charming, always the life of the party. She has his aquamarine eyes and wide white smile. That day, he would have been so proud of the loving woman she had become. I hoped that he could see from heaven.

Timidly, Katherine and Machenta scattered the rose petals down the aisle and took their places next to me.

Then Melissa glided down the aisle on our mother's arm. She looked stunning and vibrant in her formal white, over-the-shoulder taffeta gown. She wore her silky blondish-brown hair wisped in a French braid. My eyes met hers. I was overcome with emotion as I reflected upon all the events that had brought us to this moment.

Melissa was forty and had never been married, despite many proposals. Tom was five years younger, and I worried that he might be too immature; but they were determined to marry, and it was happening. In just minutes, she would officially be a wife and a stepmother.

Our passionate pastor, Jack Noble, performed the ceremony. After, he looked at Tom from beneath thick, bushy, ink-black eyebrows and said, "Now for the moment you have been waiting for. You may kiss the bride."

Tom smiled, lifted Melissa's veil, and romantically pulled her close and kissed her.

As Tom and Melissa strode back down the petal-covered aisle, it appeared as if they were floating, like in a fairy tale. I nudged the girls to join their groomsmen and follow down the aisle, and I walked outside to meet CH.

CH picked me up in the car, and we sped off to reach the yacht ahead of the guests. We had only a few minutes to set out the place cards and check all the arrangements.

Tom, Melissa, and Mom arrived first. Tom approached CH and asked, "Hey, could you videotape during the reception? My sister was supposed to do it, but she's uncomfortable with the camera. It's easy to operate. Let me show you how it works." Although CH had never used this video camera before, he graciously agreed to do his best. As an engineer, CH was gifted at managing any left-brain maneuver with finesse. As the yacht cruised past mile after mile of luxurious estates and swaying grand palm trees alongside the Intracoastal Waterway, CH interacted with guests to capture the essence of the floating reception.

Everyone was dancing, and I even began to sway to the music. I longed to dance and wished that I could share a slow dance with CH. Melissa instructed the DJ to play my favorite song, "Somewhere over the Rainbow." As I headed in CH's direction, Melissa's best friend, Ernie, intercepted and asked me to dance.

Ernie is a great-looking, accomplished Lebanese man. Instantly, he made me laugh with his quick wit. He and his perky, petite wife, Rachel, are longtime friends who had provided unwavering support during my accident and recovery. As Ernie led me across the dance floor in his tux and tails, I was dancing close to CH in my imagination. I was disappointed that I never got to dance with CH before the reception ended.

When the last guests departed, CH and I gathered our things, headed for the car, and drove to the Embassy Suites to join Melissa and Tom for a nightcap.

Finally heading home to the condo, we drove down the A1A by the ocean. This was one of my favorite routes because the Intracoastal Waterway was on the west side and the east side was home to posh, exquisitely landscaped, oceanfront villas. In the moonlight, it was romantic. We opened the sunroof and enjoyed the soft breeze and starlit sky.

When we reached the condo, CH parked and helped me carry in all the stuff we'd accumulated at the wedding and reception. Inside the condo, CH collapsed on the contemporary sectional, loosened his tie, and took off his jacket. "I can't wait to take off these shoes," I said. "They're killing my feet." I climbed onto the matching chaise lounge next to him. I was exhausted but didn't want this enchanting evening to ever end.

I turned to CH and said, "I have a dreadful secret. Finally, I can tell someone."

He gave me his full attention.

"Two months ago, I found out that I have a lump in my left breast. I didn't want to spoil the wedding or to have the focus of attention shift from Melissa to me, so I haven't told anyone. I can't conceive that I might have breast cancer after everything

I've been through. I don't think I could endure chemotherapy or radiation with all my existing health issues. I'm scheduled to have a biopsy when Melissa returns from her honeymoon."

CH stood, nestled back down beside me, and held me close. "Try not to worry. Hopefully, it will be benign." His body felt warm and firm pressed next to mine. His tender expression, soft voice, and reassuring embrace comforted me. He stayed close for several minutes, and then he returned to the sectional. I thought he may have been thinking of kissing me, but he didn't.

"I'm uncomfortable getting involved in a relationship until my divorce is finalized," he said. "It should be over soon." Shortly after that he left.

I felt disappointed yet encouraged. His comment implied that he was considering a relationship with me. Perhaps he still thought of me as a best friend or a sister. How could I expect him to be physically attracted to me with my disfigurement?

Monday morning, we drove to the Fort Lauderdale airport, and as we approached the entrance, my heart sank. I didn't want him to leave. We parked, and I watched his every move in the rearview mirror as he unloaded his bags. I got out of the car to move to the driver's side.

After retrieving his bag from the trunk, he gave me a tight, big hug and said, "I'm so glad I could be here. I had a great time. Take care of yourself. I'll call you soon."

I fought back tears. I hated goodbyes, especially this one. "I couldn't have done all of this without your help. Thank you for being here. I'm going to miss you."

I lingered to watch him as he entered the terminal. He looked back, smiled, and waved. Tears streaked down my face and blurred my vision as I drove away, alone and in love.

CHAPTER TWENTY-TWO

A Thanksgiving Twist

*Sometimes good things fall apart so better
things can fall together.*

Marilyn Monroe

After Melissa's wedding

After I broke up with Alex, he continued to send letters and
expressed his disappointment and desire to remain friends. I
agreed to give friendship a try. Before we realized it, we'd convinced ourselves that our romantic relationship was too precious to dismiss without trying again. We resumed the calls,
letters, and cards, but the spark was little more than a glimmer
fighting to keep its glow.

Meanwhile, CH continued to call more often and sent
thoughtful and humorous cards to encourage me. Thanksgiving was approaching, and Alex was supposed to come to Fort
Lauderdale. I didn't want him to come, but I didn't want to hurt
him. I didn't have the heart to tell him not to visit. Conversations that had been spontaneous and fun became strained and

trite. Alex sensed my distance and called me the Monday before Thanksgiving. He said, "Under the circumstances, I don't think I should make the trip. I don't feel like you really want me to come."

Silence. I inhaled a deep breath and said, "Alex, I'm so sorry, but we can't seem to recover the love we once had. We've tried, but it's just not there anymore."

"I still don't understand what happened and why you fell out of love with me."

"I'm sorry. I can't change the way I feel." I didn't want to tell him that he had helped me to discover that rather than a burn survivor, I wanted a man whose health suggested that not every aspect of our joint existence needed to be defined by burn injuries and their resultant disfigurement and challenges.

And I had a very particular man in mind.

Tuesday night, I called CH and said, "What are you doing for Thanksgiving?"

"I'm planning to have lunch with your mom and James."

"Have you bought yourself a Christmas present?"

"Why do you ask?" he said.

"Why don't you come to Fort Lauderdale for Thanksgiving?"

There was just enough silence on the other end of the line to make my heart race. Then he said, "Let's do it!"

"Wonderful, I'll check out the flights and prices and call you back. It may be pricey because it's so late and a holiday weekend."

"Let's see what we can find."

I called him back with the information, and he booked the flight. I was a nervous wreck from that moment until I picked him up at the airport. We had become best friends, and I didn't want to jeopardize that but felt compelled to keep an open mind to other possibilities. Would I be comfortable with him in the condo for four days, or would it be awkward? Where would he sleep?

Anxiously, on Thanksgiving day, I drove to the Fort Lauderdale airport to get him. We went to Deerfield Beach, had lunch, and then spent the day with Melissa, Tom, and his daughters. CH fit in, and Melissa and Tom treated him like he was part of the family. When we returned to the condo that evening, I showed him to the guest bedroom and bath and told him I was beat. It was clear that he was, too. I told him to make himself at home. "I'm glad that you're here."

"Me, too. I'll see you in the morning."

On Friday night, we had tickets to a fabulous concert in West Palm Beach, "Colors of Christmas," starring Peabo Bryson and Melissa Manchester. Initially, I had bought only three tickets but, luckily, had found a single ticket about eight rows behind our seats for CH. Tom and Melissa picked us up. After dinner at one of our favorite restaurants, we headed for the Kravis Center for the Performing Arts. We arrived at the impressive theater, which had a stunning atrium and windows from the floor to the ceiling. People clad in festive, elegant attire were sipping champagne as they chatted before the concert. Gorgeous poinsettias announced the arrival of Christmastime. There was an air of excitement and the feeling of Christmas. We made our way up the spiral staircase to our seats. I wished that CH could sit next to me, but he was so gracious and understanding, happy just to be there. Several times during the concert, he left his seat, came down, and stooped beside me.

Listening to some of my favorite songs from Christmas, such as "I'll Be Home for Christmas" and "The Christmas Song," made me feel sentimental and nostalgic. I was elated that CH was there with us. We had a fabulous time at the concert and chatted about the music and artists during the drive home.

That night, as I lay in bed, knowing that he was in the other bedroom, I wondered if he was thinking about being with me, or was he content to stay in the guest bedroom? At that moment, he appeared in my doorway and said, "May I join you?"

"I'd like that."

He walked over and sat down on the bed. He took off his glasses and placed them on the nightstand. Without them, he transformed into a different, sensuous man, like Clark Kent when he removed his street clothes and donned the Superman costume. He was deliberate and gentle, no longer shy or timid, but confident and virile as he pressed his lips to mine and began kissing and touching me. It was evident that more than anything, he wanted to bring me pleasure as he explored every curve and crease of my body with his fingertips. Although most of my trunk and back had served as donor sites for other parts of my body, I still had normal sensation in those areas. So I felt his warm, soft fingers with each caress. As he kissed my neck, I became more aroused. His body next to mine was hot and firm. Passion intoxicated me, and I became lost in our lovemaking—lost in a way that led me to forget about my burned skin and disfigurement. The ecstasy was ethereal, not simply a manifestation of two physical beings having sex. Like the sky over Cat Island, lovemaking with CH was dimensionless.

CHAPTER TWENTY-THREE

A Botched Investigation

*I have come to believe that one thing people
cannot bear is a sense of injustice. Poverty,
cold, even hunger, are more bearable than
injustice.*

Millicent Fenwick

Three and a half years after the crash

The day after the accident, Jack Kihm and Bill Skellenger visited
the crash site. They were shocked to discover that no one was
on site investigating—not the Federal Aviation Administration
(FAA), the Civil Aviation Authority Bahamas (CAAB), the US
National Transportation Safety Board (NTSB), or anyone. The
debris and remnants of the airplane, all essential to the investigation, lay on the ground, available for anyone to take or to be
damaged by wind and sand. Nathaniel had salvaged and stored
some parts of the plane. In the days following the accident, the
aircraft manufacturer initiated an extensive investigation, as
did the manufacturer of the engines.

I asked my attorney at the time, Barry Meadow, "Why isn't the FAA or NTSB investigating the accident?"

"Because the crash occurred outside of the US."

"But they investigate crashes all the time involving planes made in America and US citizens. Why not this crash?"

"The NTSB deferred the investigation to the Bahamas aviation authority." Pierre Dupuch, minister of consumer welfare and aviation in the Bahamas, headed the investigation.

As a citizen of the US, I felt cheated and disappointed by the NTSB. We deserved to have a thorough, impartial investigation of our crash by the preeminent aviation experts of the NTSB. A comprehensive, timely investigation might have produced invaluable evidence. Instead, the NTSB *Preliminary Aviation Report* was filed solely for informational purposes and contained only the information provided by or requested by the Bahamian aviation authorities who were investigating the accident. The three-page report filed by the director general of CAAB had several errors, including the accident and rescue date. The report said that we were evacuated by a US Coast Guard aircraft to Miami. The report noted that the flight originated from Miami. How could any of the findings discovered by the Bahamian authorities be trusted when the most basic facts were erroneously reported?

Apparently, it didn't matter to the NTSB, the FAA, or any agency that our plane had crashed, that Roger had died, and that I had been critically injured.

Mr. Dupuch called me four months after my initial request for a report of the accident. His response was "there is no report." They didn't think I was going to live and never bothered to investigate the crash until I called to request a copy of the report! For months, I had been waiting to hear from them. With that news, anger swelled within me until I was nauseated with rage. For the first time in my life, I understood how some sane, decent, honorable people are driven to do outrageous, violent things in times of absolute desperation. I would never have believed that I could express the emotions that now riveted my entire being. Just how much is one person supposed to be able to endure before snapping? *Breathe, just breathe deeply, and concentrate on calming down to regain your composure.* Emotionally, I felt like I was weakening, exhausted from the constant struggle in every area of my life. I continued to pray that God would give me the strength to keep fighting. I thanked God for bringing CH into my life. His quiet and gentle ways soothed my anguished soul like a cool breeze blowing across the ocean into my window, across my face and body.

During the early stage of the investigation, the airplane's manufacturer claimed that the aircraft had been overloaded and contained hazardous materials, such as a propane tank, a five-gallon can of paint, and a motorcycle. Since the plane was already loaded when I boarded that fateful day, I had no recollection of what was on board, except for luggage, camera equipment, groceries, and a handcrafted wooden chair that I had bought from one of the showrooms at DCOTA.

Unlike Mr. Meadow's firm, which initially investigated the crash and attributed primarily pilot error to the cause of the accident, I was positive the crash was not Roger's fault. I knew that mechanics had worked to repair the recurrent problem with the landing gear and position indicator light. The mechanics who had worked on the airplane insisted that the problem was electrical, related to the right indicator light that affirms that the right main landing gear is securely locked in the extended position. On several occasions, I had witnessed the green indicator light failing to illuminate when Roger attempted to lower and lock the landing gear. In those instances, we were on approach to land at the airport in Rock Sound, where air traffic control personnel could view the plane during a go-around to visually confirm that the right landing gear was down, but not that it was locked in the down position. Ironically, never once while landing in Fort Lauderdale had we experienced this problem.

Each time we had a problem with the right landing gear, Roger expressed anger and frustration with the maintenance company for not fixing it. Upon returning to Fort Lauderdale, Roger would again report the problem and inform the mechanics that the malfunction was not with the indicator light but with the landing gear itself. He didn't spare any words to express his displeasure. Once, after we had just returned from Cat Island and landed in Fort Lauderdale, he taxied to the private jetport where we deplaned. We grabbed our bags and headed inside. Roger walked over to the representative on duty, and in a stern voice, he said, "You can ask those fellows how they'd like to be sitting in the cockpit when one of the landing gears doesn't lock. How would they like to land that plane on an unmanned runway in the Bahamas? I'm tired of this shit. Fix the problem!"

More than three years had lapsed since the black plumes of smoke had covered the sky over the crash site on Cat Island. Yet, in October 1997, I continued to search for another attorney who was an expert in aviation litigation and who believed the crash was caused by a mechanical failure and not solely by pilot error.

The crash on Cat Island

According to an article in the *Washington Post* (Phillips, 1999), the NTSB and the Aircraft Owners and Pilots Association (AOPA) estimate that 71 percent of fatal crashes/ aviation accidents are pilot related but that 14.1 percent are maintenance related. The latter statistic seemed to be overlooked by most of the attorneys whom I contacted.

Could Roger have made a better decision on that fateful day? I didn't know, but I was positive he didn't cause the crash. However, if I was going to file a suit, I was running out of time. The statute of limitations was fast approaching. My dear friend and fellow burn survivor George Pessotti encouraged me to not give up on finding an attorney. He had spoken to several on my behalf. Still, unfortunately, none of them agreed to represent me because of the investment in time and resources required to investigate an out-of-state and offshore accident and because of speculation that the cause was pilot error. Why did so many of the attorneys concur that this accident resulted from pilot error? "Pilot error" unequivocally blamed Roger for negligence. Or had Roger lied all those months? Had he adequately maintained the airplane?

Most legal firms lacked aviation expertise, and some believed the lawsuit was too risky. My dear friend and notable trial attorney in Michigan, Rick Halpert, championed my case and introduced me to David Katzman, one of the world's preeminent aviation attorneys and aviation law experts. He began flying at age fourteen and was an active pilot with thousands of hours of flying multiple aircraft types. With extensive litigation experience in complex personal injury, wrongful death, and commercial product liability claims, he had an impressive record of successful verdicts and settlements. David was licensed to practice in Florida, and he held an Airline Transport Pilot certificate from the FAA, which is the equivalent of a doctorate degree in flying. We talked by phone, and afterward, he said that he wanted to meet me in person.

My first face-to-face meeting with David Katzman was early on a cold, sunny Saturday morning in 1997 in a small, stark waiting room of a private jetport in Greensboro. CH accompanied me inside. Outside the room full of windows, I noticed a corporate jet parked nearby.

David, a man of small stature, nicely dressed, looked at CH and said, "Could you step outside the room so that I can talk in private with Ms. Pell?"

"Sure, I'll be happy to," CH said as he walked out of the room and closed the door.

David got right to the point. Staring directly into my eyes, he said, "This will be a very tough case to prove because much of the key evidence is missing, but I believe your story, and there have been similar accidents caused by mechanical problems. Sadly, Roger may have jeopardized the case with some of his actions. You, certainly, were harmed through no fault of your own, and if you want me to represent you, I'll do my best to see that you receive compensation for your extensive losses. My fee is forty percent."

For the first time in more than three long and trying years, I felt as if someone outside of my immediate circle believed that the crash was not caused solely by pilot error and was willing and capable of proving it.

"Yes, I absolutely want you to represent me. Thank you so much for taking my case."

"It's going to be a long, tedious, stressful ordeal, but hopefully, we'll be successful. My assistant will contact you next week to start the process. Now I've got to run."

As he was about to walk away, I said, "All the money in the world can't restore my body or bring back Roger, but it could make my life more bearable."

He hustled to the private jet, climbed the entry stairs, and disappeared inside the cockpit. I was surprised to see that he was piloting the company jet. I smiled with joy and excitement. Maybe David could prove that the landing gear caused the crash, and the companies liable for the mechanical failure and botched repairs would be held accountable for their actions. I was filled with hope. I walked into another section of the building and found CH patiently reading a magazine. CH loved airplanes. He had dreamed of becoming a pilot, but his poor eyesight disqualified him. As I approached, he looked up from the magazine and smiled.

"How did it go?"

"Great! Let's get out of here, and I'll tell you all about it."

Hand in hand, we walked outdoors to the parking lot, climbed into CH's van, and headed out.

"David wasn't too happy to see that I had a boyfriend. He implied that a jury would be more sympathetic if I appeared unloved and alone. Plus, he was suspicious of your motives!"

"Wow, that's awful."

"I made it clear that you were an essential part of my life, and I had no intention of postponing my life until the lawsuit was over. I think he understood."

"You know that I would never want to do anything that might jeopardize your chance of receiving compensation for your injuries."

"I know, sweetie, let's not worry about that. David has lots of more important issues to deal with right now. You're the best part of my life. I'm not about to postpone our relationship."

CH reached over to hold my hand as we drove back toward town.

To my surprise, David discovered that there had been a very superficial, mismanaged, inadequate investigation of the crash by my first attorney. To make matters worse, I learned that it was already too late to gather crucial evidence, eyewitness testimony, and information. In addition, the memories of those involved had lost their sharp focus. The lack of such direct evidence could mean the difference between my winning or losing the lawsuit.

David hired Donald Sommer, a renowned aircraft crash investigator. They flew to Cat Island, rented a large International Harvester front loader, and together set about locating as much of the wreckage as possible to try to piece together the cause of the crash. They found parts from the airplane scattered over Cat Island, many at the local garbage dump (which they picked through), and others around the accident site. David rented storage space on Cat Island and put the evidence they gathered under lock and key. Still, nearly four years had passed, and many of the airplane's parts were not located, including elements from the landing gear.

Just in time, we filed lawsuits against the manufacturers of the airplane and the engines—one day before the statute of limitations would have expired!

Nearly five years after the crash, I was deposed. I was

nervous because David had cautioned me that the defense lawyer would twist my testimony and do his best to intimidate and confuse me, but he had reassured me that he would be by my side to object to any inappropriate or irrelevant questions. One of the most irritating aspects of the questioning was when the defendants' attorney asked me for specific dates of incidences that had happened five years earlier.

As I listened to and watched David during the deposition, I understood why he was such a successful attorney. I knew that he was the best attorney to represent me. This reassured me and renewed my hope.

The day after the deposition, during my session with Dr. Mic, I told him the stress was unbearable. "The lawsuit, rehab, ongoing operations—it's too much."

He leaned forward and said, "Whenever negative thoughts flood your mind, take some deep breaths and shift your attention to something else. Or take a break, listen to some relaxing music, or read a book or magazine."

"It's unnerving when the defendants' attorney questions my integrity, my motives!"

"Try to depersonalize the situation and remember that the defense attorney's job is to do everything possible to discredit you and your testimony."

"I know, but it still hurts and makes me furious."

"That's what the defense attorney wants. So don't take the bait."

"I'll do my best. I'll be glad when this nightmare is over."

For months following my deposition, friends, family members, and Roger's employees were deposed, as well as representatives for the defendants. One witness for the plane's manufacturer contended that Roger hadn't properly maintained the airplane by failing to have it inspected in a timely fashion, and that he had landed short of the runway, causing the landing gear to collapse when it struck a berm of sand just in front of the runway threshold. I knew this was not true. An employee for the airplane maintenance company had worked on the landing gear, trying to identify and repair the ongoing problem, and this company was the sole entity involved in servicing the airplane. Multiple repair invoices from the defendant detailed the mechanic's failed attempts and inability to repair the landing gear.

Importantly, on the rescue flight to Miami, Roger had said, "I just paid twenty-five hundred bucks to fix the landing gear."

My legal team contradicted the airplane manufacturer's report and showed that other crashes of the same model of airplane had occurred because of landing gear malfunctions. The litigation continued until the summer of 2000, when we reached an out-of-court settlement. A settlement is a compromise, a guarantee of receiving something less than full compensation while eliminating the risk of receiving nothing. David thought going to trial was too risky when measured against the amount of money the defendants would pay for the settlement. David believed the jury would blame Roger for most of the fault for the crash. Knowing that the landing gear extension and locked indicator light had not illuminated earlier in Rock Sound, clearly indicating a problem with the landing gear, Roger had attempted to land at a remote, unmanned island airport without emergency equipment. It turned out that Roger was underinsured, and his estate could not pay for his fault for the accident. One of the most important witnesses from the maintenance company reported that he had refused to "sign off" on the last repair regarding the landing gear and indicator light but later said that he would not testify.

My first attorney had discovered that Roger was having financial problems. I was shocked to learn this; I had never seen any indication of money trouble from Roger's spending habits or our lifestyle. I knew he had recently obtained a $50,000 business loan, but that didn't seem out of the ordinary. The settlement of his estate revealed that he had considerable debt. I wondered why he had never mentioned this to me.

CHAPTER TWENTY-FOUR

A New Purpose and Passion

One knows what one has lost, but not what one may find.

George Sand

Four and a half years after the crash

A few weeks after giving the homily at St. Maurice Catholic Church, I joined the Florida Speakers Association, attended monthly meetings, and became a National Speakers Association member. As a member of this outstanding professional organization, I traveled to national conferences where I learned the best practices for speaking, like limiting the number of points per speech to three, pausing to emphasize a point, and using humor to relax the audience.

I began speaking at churches, universities, corporations, and civic organizations in South Florida. I organized and presented at the first reunion of burn survivors in South Florida in cooperation with Jackson Memorial Hospital. I talked to regional university occupational and physical therapy students about burn care from a patient's perspective.

In 1998, Dr. Michael Peck, who had left Jackson Memorial to become medical director of the North Carolina Jaycee Burn Center, invited me to speak at the Burn Center's annual reunion of patients and health care providers. My speech was titled "Do the Thing You Think You Cannot Do." I shared with the audience the resources that gave me insight into challenges, alleviated stress and anxiety, motivated or inspired me, and provided psychological and emotional relief.

I emphasized how essential it had been to accept my disfigured face and body to move forward and find meaning in life. It was unproductive and drained my energy and spirit to focus on the past, what might have been, or all I had lost.

I told them that smooth jazz by musicians like Earl Klugh and George Winston soothed my soul and calmed my anxiety. Inspirational books like *Still Me* by Christopher Reeve, *Head First* by Norman Cousins, *Hope for the Troubled Heart* by Billy Graham, and *All Things Are Possible Through Prayer* by Charles L. Allen had taught me essential coping skills and had provided insight into life's most formidable challenges.

Man's Search for Meaning by Viktor Frankl had a profound effect on me. Initially, after the crash, seeing my body reminded me of the horrific photographs of prisoners in the concentration camps during the Holocaust. Knowing that some of those starved and tortured people had survived their unthinkable ordeal gave me hope that I, too, could survive.

Norman Cousins, author of *Anatomy of an Illness* and many other books about the biology of hope and the healing power of the human spirit, wrote in *Head First*: "The ultimate tragedy is to die without discovering the possibilities of full growth." Today there is accumulating proof for Cousins's premise that hope, faith, laughter, and the will to live are related to biochemical factors that can help combat serious disease.

It's important for all of us to have role models to help us navigate unfamiliar territory. Christopher Reeve was my first hero after my injury. I knew exactly what he meant by "still me," the title of his memoir. He, too, was trapped in a different body, but he was the same remarkable man. Of course, society treated him and me differently once we became "out of the ordinary."

After he was thrown headfirst from his horse in an accident that broke his neck and left him unable to move or breathe, he never allowed his paralysis to define or deter him from accomplishing groundbreaking work and living the best life possible.

Kevin Michael Connolly also inspired me; he was born without legs, yet he placed second in the winter X Games and used his prize money to travel to thirteen countries and thirty-three cities. He used a skateboard as his local transportation. While traveling, Kevin snapped thirty-three thousand photographs of people staring at him! He said that the one thing that all the people staring had in common was their look of disdain. His photographs have appeared in major museums across the country.

James Partridge, founder of Changing Faces, and Alan Breslau, founder of the Phoenix Society for Burn Survivors, were two of my favorite role models. They both had sustained severe, disfiguring burn injuries, yet they had applied their experience and expertise to helping others with disfiguring conditions. They transformed adversity into an adventure beyond their imaginations, helping thousands of individuals reclaim their lives.

Our frame of mind and thoughts direct our destiny and determine whether we survive tragedies and disappointments or succumb to them as victims. How we think about our situation shapes the outcome. If we allow ourselves to become "stuck" in the past, dwelling on what might have been, we will never enter the present. We will overlook the possibilities and opportunities that unfold before us.

Over the years, I have witnessed the power of positive, hopeful thinking. It's unstoppable, but so is the force of limited, fearful thought. One opens doors; the other slams doors and steals opportunities. It's all up to us; we get to choose the direction, to move forward with faith and hope, or linger in a mire of helplessness and disappointment. There's considerable research to prove that the way we think affects outcomes.

Resilience is vital to surviving and recovering from unexpected injuries, illnesses, setbacks, and disappointments. Some people appear to be born with this gift; others acquire it through life experience. Either we choose to move forward in the face of adversity or remain "in place" or "stuck" where we are. Resilience is the ability to fall down or fail but not judge or define ourselves by a single situation or misstep. Instead, we can learn to "bounce forward."

I described how yoga and massage stretched my taut, contracted skin and how exercise improved my energy and mood. Guided imagery is a type of deliberate, directed daydreaming, a relaxed concentration proven to alleviate pain, depression, anxiety, and phobias. The program intertwines mind and body principles and uses senses and memory to engage the imagination. Combined with breathing and touch, the program continues to help me manage pain, anxiety, anger, forgiveness, and trauma. I learned how to avoid fighting with or being angry with my pain. Belleruth's dreamy, gentle voice transported me to a safe, relaxed, pain-free state of being.

Diet, nutrition, and rest contributed to my healing and renewal. I found solace in quotes and scripture, like "What does not kill me makes me stronger" by Nietzsche and "But with God all things are possible" (Matthew 19:26). Every morning and evening, I read the Nietzsche quote out loud. As a Christian, it bothered me that I derived so much strength and determination from such an anti-Christian source, but my life seems to have proven that God indeed works in mysterious ways.

I discussed my renewed faith and how prayer helped me endure grueling pain, discomfort, and agitation. Attending church gave me hope and eased stress and anxiety. Every morning, before getting out of bed, I thanked God for my mom, Melissa, friends, and caregivers and for another day to see, smell, hear, touch, taste, walk, and pursue new dreams. Nightly, before going to sleep, I closed my eyes and said, "Lord, thank you for this day of life."

Distraction was one of the most effective means of managing pain. Time evaporated whenever I was writing, researching, or working on a project. I talked about the importance to me of the sacrifices, support, and reassurance provided, with love, by my mom and sister and the cards, calls, and visits from friends and associates.

One of the most inspiring forms of hope came from befriending another burn survivor with similar injuries, Kevin McGann. I first met Kevin when he and his petite, feisty wife stopped by my room at the rehab hospital. I learned that Mom and Melissa had met Nancy in the waiting room at the Burn Center and that they had instantly bonded. They were all dealing with the horror of what had happened to us, adjusting to our nearly unrecognizable appearances and life-threatening injuries. The endless stress, anxiety, uncertainty, and angst they'd felt while tethered to the hospital waiting room for so many months, juggling their own lives and responsibilities in addition to attending to our needs, had brought them together.

Once Kevin could walk alone, he stopped by my room often. He always greeted me with the exact same words: "Hey, baby, how ya doing today?" His head was bandaged and covered by a bandana, and he had burns on much of his face and most of his body, but his winning smile was a refreshing and welcome sight. Kevin gave me hope because I witnessed his gradual progress. Our burns were very similar. I knew that if he could do something, I most likely would be able to do the same thing in time. (Yes, "in time"—eventually, even I started saying it.) We felt an instant bond of respect and care for one another.

We were kindred spirits on a long, painful journey of recovery and rehabilitation, and we understood exactly what the other person was feeling, physically and emotionally. Unlike me, Kevin still had his beloved spouse to lean on through the long, grueling process. Nancy cheered him on every day.

I learned that Kevin had an identical twin. I could only imagine the agonizing heartache that Nancy must experience whenever she sees Kevin's brother, or how Kevin feels, looking at his reflection in his brother's face. I only have photographs of myself before the accident to remind me of the "other" me. Nancy has a live replica of her husband to remind her of how handsome he was.

I discussed the anxiety, pain, and suffering of spouses and loved ones of burn survivors. In most instances, their lives were also upended emotionally, psychologically, socially, and financially. It is agonizing to sit in waiting areas for the latest update on a loved one's condition or to find out if a procedure was successful. Worst of all, a surgeon could appear and ask to see family members in a private room to tell them that their loved one didn't survive. It is all-consuming and exhausting to care for a burn survivor.

Melissa had told me how, several times during my hospitalization, burn surgeons had escorted Mom and her into a private room and said, "You need to prepare yourself for the possibility that Charlene won't live through this surgery. She's endured so much." Unmoved by their warning, Melissa would say, "You don't know my sister. She's the strongest person I've ever known. She's going to make it through this and all the surgeries. She's a fighter!"

I found a quote by Albert Schweitzer in Norman Cousins's book *Anatomy of an Illness* that eloquently describes the feeling between Kevin and me and our loved ones: "There is a fellowship among those who bear the mark of pain." Cousins added, "Those outside the fellowship have great difficulty understanding what lies beneath the pain." I found this fellowship on a much larger scale when I discovered hundreds of burn survivors through the Phoenix Society. It's invaluable to find a support group, to meet with others who share similar conditions, challenges, and concerns.

I closed my speech with this quote by Charles L. Allen:

> *It is so easy to feel that everything is lost, that life from now on will not be worth living. But it may be—it often is—that which we thought was the setting of the sun may be the sunrise. There may be more light ahead than we thought possible. What seemed to be the end may be a new beginning (in Robert J. Mueller's The Gentle Art of Caring).*

This speech set me on a new course of speaking and consulting primarily with burn survivors, health care professionals at burn center retreats and reunions, and the annual WBC hosted by the Phoenix Society. It was especially rewarding to conduct a workshop at the WBC. I had come full circle. I was in a position to help other survivors adapt to their changed appearance and circumstances. I could share my experience and insights and give them the hope that had once been given to me at my first WBC.

One of the issues that I discuss with health care professionals is how demoralizing and upsetting it was to rely on the assistance of a caregiver or family member to perform basic hygiene maneuvers like brushing my teeth, blowing my nose, and more-personal acts. I ask them, "Have you ever asked someone else to feed you or brush your teeth, to see what it feels like? Experiencing this firsthand will give you a better understanding of what your patients are going through."

I encourage caregivers to listen to their patients and involve them in their recovery. Often, patients devise creative solutions to their physical challenges. Heterotrophic ossification in my elbows prevented me from bending my elbows enough to reach my toothbrush to my mouth with a standard toothbrush; I asked my dear friend Debra to buy some chopsticks so that we could tape my toothbrush to the chopstick to create a longer handle. The extended handle enabled me to brush my teeth unassisted. This gave me a tiny bit of control, independence, and hope. I asked Melissa to try the same trick with a fork and spoon. It worked, and I could feed myself. That was a pivotal occasion and cause to celebrate!

My creativity and resourcefulness came in handy during rehabilitation. I have always loved art and design. Once, I had used a hole puncher to gather hundreds of tiny, round pieces of colored paper to meticulously create a rendition of Vincent van Gogh's *The Starry Night*. It required hours of sorting the pieces of paper into similar colors and painstakingly gluing paper dots in a pattern that replicated the painting. I delighted in creating art out of ordinary materials.

In 1986, when I started designing and making jewelry, I used beads, brass washers from the hardware store, and all sorts of doodads typically used to make fishing lures to create unique earrings. Years later, I was elated to read in Ray Bradbury's book *Yestermorrow* that he envisioned such jewelry in the hardware stores of the future. I invited this brilliant, acclaimed author and visionary to be the keynote speaker for the annual design conference at DCOTA the year before the crash.

I shared with health care providers what a perceptive champion for the poor and medically underserved, Dr. Ron Anderson, chairman of the board of Parkland hospital in Dallas, wrote: "Traditionally, hospitals are organized for doctors, auxiliaries, and insurance companies—everybody but the patient" (quoted in Alan Bryson's *Healing Mind, Body & Soul*). While burn patients benefit from the sterile hospital environment, they suffer from the lack of colors and textures that define the comforts of home. The unfamiliar sounds of the medical equipment monitoring their vitals can frighten and startle with their beeps and alarms. And given their fragile condition, the moans of others in pain may feel like too much to bear. The scents of alcohol, urine, and cleaning solutions, as well as the indescribable but recognizable scent of illness, cannot be escaped. Stripped of our own clothing, significant personal belongings, and large swaths of our skin, we are rendered entirely vulnerable.

By sharing these insights, I trusted that others might find hope and optimism in the face of suffering and despair. I had a new purpose and passion that fueled me with the energy and determination to improve burn care and the resources to help burn survivors adjust and adapt to their changed appearance, unimaginable losses, and formidable circumstances.

CHAPTER TWENTY-FIVE

One Red Rose

One love, one heart, one destiny.

Bob Marley

Almost five years after the crash

Thanksgiving Eve, CH and I had just returned from Tom and Melissa's house. We pulled into the parking garage, parked, and walked inside to the elevators. I punched the button for the eighteenth floor. "I don't think we could have squeezed another thing into this day. I'm exhausted."

"Your mom seems so happy to be here. It's a shame that she and Melissa have to live so far apart."

"And ironic that we both live here now because of my accident. Mom loves being around Tom's girls. She's given up on having any maternal grandchildren."

At Melissa's house, Katherine and Machenta had created an assortment of holiday decorations for the dining room and table. They made American Indian headpieces from brown paper bags painted orange, yellow, brown, and red. They cut out place cards in the shapes of leaves from brightly colored construction paper and wrote our names on them. The girls' decorations and the aromas of rosemary, cinnamon, and turkey from the kitchen carried the promise of Thanksgiving.

"It never really feels like Thanksgiving or Christmas in Florida," I said. "I so miss the autumn leaves and cooler weather."

CH and I were happy to be back in the condo, in peace.

"How about a nightcap?" I asked.

"That sounds great. What are you having?"

"I'm thinking of a Baileys and coffee. What would you like?"

"A nutty Irishman would be awesome."

Since a weekend getaway to the Grove Park Inn in Asheville, CH loved a nutty Irishman. I vividly recalled that weekend because I remembered the disappointment I experienced while eating lunch at a restaurant veranda overlooking the Appalachian Mountains. The fall foliage was breathtaking, and the air felt crisp and fresh. After lunch, CH reached into his jacket pocket and pulled out a small black box that I hoped might be an engagement ring. I opened it with anticipation and discovered a lovely silver bracelet. I'd struggled to hide my disappointment.

"Thank you, it's beautiful. Here, help me put it on."

"It looked unique, like something you would like. I found it at the museum gallery gift shop that you love."

I smiled as I admired the bracelet on my wrist, while thinking that this romantic, scenic vista would have been the perfect place and moment to pop the question. But he didn't. I wondered if he would ever ask me to marry him.

My thoughts returned to our busy day, and we collapsed on the sofa and enjoyed our drinks as we listened to the smooth jazz of Boney James's Christmas music.

"Well, we better get you to bed," he said. "Tomorrow will be a long day."

"I still have to make a carrot soufflé and the cranberry sauce. So let's get up by six."

"Sounds like a plan."

I walked into the bedroom to undress and prepare for bed. I removed my makeup, washed my face, brushed and flossed my teeth, and slipped into my pajamas. I snuggled under the covers and was about to turn out the light when CH entered the bedroom. He walked over to my side of the bed, knelt on one knee, and presented me with an artificial long-stemmed red rose. The rosebud was a tiny box. He opened the box and said, "Will you marry me?"

I saw an elegant ring with many small diamonds set together to form three rows. It was perfect. I smiled with delight and said, "Of course, I'll marry you, but why did you wait until I got undressed and removed all my makeup before asking me?"

"You're beautiful to me, just the way you are."

Christmas remains my favorite holiday, but Thanksgiving Eve is my favorite day. It was another ordinary day when an unexpected event irrevocably changed my life in a divine, positive way. It marked the beginning of an extraordinary love and life with CH.

On April 24, 1999, we married at a stately home on the Intracoastal Waterway in Fort Lauderdale, Florida. CH never took his eyes off me as he escorted me down the aisle to the front of the room. He looked so handsome in his black-and-silver diamond-checkered vest and black tuxedo. His salt-and-pepper hair was striking next to the silver and black colors. I wore a sophisticated ivory trumpet gown with lace from the top of the high-neck silhouette, down the unlined back, to the skirt. I wore a pearl headband in my layered auburn hair. I carried an elegant bouquet of calla lilies, white roses, variegated ivy, Queen Anne's lace, and lilies of the valley. Their fragrant scent filled the air.

Our wedding, April 24, 1999

CJ, my former administrative assistant at DCOTA and a friend, played the flute with a small chamber ensemble that performed Pachelbel's Canon as we walked to the altar.

Six months pregnant, Melissa stood by my side in a sage floor-length dress with a cowl neck. Mom's tears showed how much the ceremony moved her. We stood beneath an ornate crystal chandelier in front of a huge fireplace. Glowing white candles, white and pink peonies, and ivy adorned the mantle. Pastors Jack Noble and Dwayne Black, both friends, performed the ceremony with tears in their eyes. Then, surrounded by family, friends, and the health care providers who had saved my life and helped me restore it, we exchanged our vows. During the ceremony, Raul Midon, who is blind, sang "Fly Me to the Moon" instead of "My One and Only You," the song planned for the ceremony. Raul couldn't see the shocked expression on my face as he performed the upbeat song intended for our first dance during the reception. CH did his best to keep his composure and smiled with love. My eyes bugged out in surprise!

And when prompted to kiss the bride, CH's lips met mine with all the warmth, richness, and love gathered in that room. All the suffering and struggle to reclaim my life converged with love to culminate in this momentous occasion—the happiest day of my life. Most likely, I would never have met or fallen in love with CH if not for the horrific burn injury and ensuing five years of pain, suffering, anxiety, and anguish. The family, friends, and caregivers gathered at our wedding had cared for and supported me through this grueling journey to reach this joyous milestone. At last, I realized my dream of loving and being loved by an extraordinary man.

Not everyone who sustains a severe, disfiguring injury is fortunate enough to find a faithful, loving, and devoted companion. I felt so blessed and excited about creating a new life with CH.

As CH's father, Hal, had said to Mom after my accident, "Doris, something good will come out of this."

Twenty-five years later, CH and I continue to share an exceptional love, relationship, and life. I manage the nonprofit I founded in 2009, Facing Forward, Inc. I help individuals with facial or physical disfigurement accept their appearance, contend with staring, communicate confidently, and advocate for face equality. CH continues to solve problems and fix almost anything, as the design engineer that he was for Ingersoll Rand for thirty-eight years. In our years together, CH has survived three types of cancer. I have been the target of several careless and reckless drivers and have endured injuries and illnesses and their related operations. Still, our love and resolve remain steadfast and enduring, just like the sturdy branches of the dogwood trees in my mom's front yard.

More in love than ever twenty-five years later!

CHAPTER TWENTY-SIX

Facing Forward

*Tolerance is the virtue that teaches us to live
with the different. It teaches us to learn from
and respect the different.*

Paulo Freire

Thirty years after the crash

Throughout forty-eight reconstructive surgeries to restore
function and improve my appearance in the first six years
after the crash, with many more since, I have pushed through
grueling physical and psychological challenges to regain a ful-
filling life. Still, I never wanted to die. There were undoubtedly many times I tried to escape the unbearable physical
pain and emotional anguish, but not by using drugs that altered my mind or dulled my senses and feelings. The fire may
have nearly destroyed my body, but my mind was intact, and I
wanted to protect it.

Several doctors said my phenomenal will to live, and something more significant than medicine, influenced my survival.

I believe the prayers of hundreds of people contributed to my survival, and God spared my life for a reason.

I found hope in these words from Joel Osteen's book *It's Your Time*, adapted from Genesis (50:20): "God, you promised what was meant for my harm you would use to my advantage. I may have been through the fire, through the famine, through the flood, but I know it's my time for your favor. It's my time to see more of your goodness in my life."

But what to do with this extraordinary second chance? Especially when it felt like years of my life had been stolen, only to suffer the stares and awkward social interactions resulting from my changed body.

People often stared at me. They still do. Guests at restaurants have asked to change their seats to avoid looking at me. Standing in lines, eyes not focused on smartphones stare at me. Airline passengers seated next to me have asked flight attendants to change their seats. Toddlers are mesmerized or frightened by me when I encounter them in public.

After my injury, I was unaware of the significant body of research about the phenomenon of staring and the stigma associated with facial disfigurement and disability. As unimaginable as it sounds, I learned that as late as the 1970s, certain states in America banned people with disabilities from public places (Rhode, 2010).

I needed to understand why people stared at others with visible differences, causing strained, uncomfortable social encounters.

I felt angry toward people who stared at me. I longed to go about my daily activities without feeling like I was in the spotlight wherever I went. I wanted to blend in. Inside my scarred body, I was the same vibrant and intelligent woman that I was before the injury. Still, all the public could see was a fragile, scarred skeleton of a woman. People stared out of shock and curiosity. They grimaced. Denied my humanness by looking away. Talked down to me. Asked prying questions. I had been instructed not to do that. In adolescence, my mom had taught me that it was rude to stare at anyone with a disability or disfigurement. Because of that strong foundation and my understanding of the research on staring, I do not allow the reactions of strangers to alter my self-confidence. Why should I let a stranger have any control over my well-being? So I learned how to contend with people who stared at me by putting strangers at ease. I took control of social situations by smiling and initiating and directing the conversation.

Building on my experience as a burn survivor and communications executive and on extensive research, I created an educational program, "What to Do When People Stare: A Workshop to Teach Individuals with Disfiguring Conditions to Contend with Staring and Improve Control of Social Interactions." This field-tested workshop educates attendees about stigma and the science of staring and explores what it feels like to be the object of stares and hurtful behavior. In addition, through specific interactive exercises, participants learn social skills to facilitate more-comfortable social interactions between nondisabled people and those with visible differences, skills they'll need to get by.

Overall, the public does not know how to interact with people who have a disability or disfigurement. No classes or programs are available to address social interaction between nondisabled people and those with a visible difference.

Research confirms that people with a disability/disfigurement typically bear the burden of managing social interactions to make nondisabled individuals feel more comfortable. But requiring the person with a visible difference to take responsibility for managing social encounters reinforces and perpetuates the dominance of nondisabled individuals over those with disabilities (Braithwaite and Thompson, 2000). Although

I choose to take responsibility to manage social interactions, I believe that, ideally, nondisabled people should share the duty.

In America, one in four people has a disability, according to recent Centers for Disease Control and Prevention data, reported in *Disability Impacts All of Us*. In addition, 70 percent of Americans will experience a temporary or permanent disability (ADA National Network, 2015).

Unintentionally, nondisabled people may show responses of confusion and avoidance (Deegan, 1977) by using nonverbal body language such as staring, grimacing, or looking away to avoid someone with a disability/disfigurement, or they may literally and figuratively talk down to someone using a wheelchair. People with facial disfigurement are often the target of intrusive stares, comments, and prying questions and report feeling uncomfortable, hurt, angry, annoyed, and rejected when strangers stare at them.

Lack of acknowledgment is also cruel because it denies humanness. Acknowledging others, especially with a smile, "makes room for them in our lives" (Hyde, 2006).

Some people treat me as if I'm invisible. This behavior is the most painful reaction because, as a total lack of acknowledgment, it disavows me as a human being. Typically, I have experienced this response in restaurant restrooms when gorgeous young women ignore me and my attempts to engage with them. A less painful form of invisibility happens when people avoid me altogether by looking away or down. Although I experience such reactions, I do not allow them to alter my self-confidence. I refuse to allow the spontaneous reactions of strangers to have any control over my well-being. I have become "staring resistant" and work to help others free themselves from the anxiety associated with social interactions. Eleanor Roosevelt said, "No one can make you feel inferior without your consent," and I agree.

I have created and led many workshops for children that

foster respect for difference and may reduce teasing and bullying. For example, the workshop "Outside, Inside; You Decide" encourages positive social behavior, integration, and inclusion. Moreover, it introduces awareness of stereotyping and discrimination. Through thought-provoking discussions and interactions that celebrate sameness and difference, students learn to recognize and value physical, cultural, and religious diversity in our world today.

More than fifteen hundred students have completed the interactive program, which aims to help them realize how important it is to form opinions based on the person—their character, personality, intellect, and sense of humor—not solely on their appearance. One of my most precious possessions is a collection of 120 letters from several classes of students at Greensboro Day School in North Carolina. An overwhelming number of the children said they would never view somebody with a facial or physical difference in the same way after completing the program. The most frequently repeated remark was similar to this student's: "I will never stare at someone who looks different again, because I found out that it is not what they look like on the outside; it's what they are on the inside." Gulnaar Kaur, another student, wrote a touching poem that captured the terror of the crash and the miracle of my survival, loss, and pain.

> What's wrong—moment of horror,
> your pilot, lover, loving, loved,
> anguish on his face,
> "Oh, no."

> Flying to the Bahamas,
> landing gear—check . . . maybe not,
> trying to pull up, hill incoming;

Trees bending, snapping,
airplane spiraling,
memories lost,
children crying;

Miracle, miracle.

Bodies burning,
who-knows-what exploding,
flames feasting, feasting.

Healing, years and years,
everlasting pain,
everlasting hope,
determination, courage;

Miracle, miracle.

Children with visible scarring often must contend with teasing, name-calling, and bullying. Such hurtful behavior affects self-esteem, confidence, and interaction with other children. It can lead to isolation, withdrawal, rejection, discrimination, and, most tragically, suicide. Children are not born biased, but they notice differences at a young age. Preschool children begin to absorb society's messages and fears. Without intervention, this may transform children's awareness into prejudice (Anti-Defamation League, 2016).

It is crucial to engage students in discussions that compare the classroom to society, to create experiences for them to learn how to respect those who are different from them and to understand social etiquette, socialization, teamwork, and trust. I agree with twentieth-century educational philosopher John Dewey that education is not just a place to learn knowledge but also a place to learn how to live.

Providing this education is ever challenging because of school funding cuts for social and emotional learning programs. With our world so full of hate, prejudice, discrimination, and intolerance for anyone different from us, such education cannot be considered nonessential. We haven't come far enough from the 1970s. Research tells us that people form opinions about each other in seven seconds, primarily based on outward appearance and nonverbal body language. According to organizations representing people with visible dermatological conditions, burns, rare diseases, craniofacial anomalies, and cancer, millions of these individuals suffer from social problems. In a society that covets and values beauty more than health, having a facial or physical disfigurement can be a significant barrier to social interaction. Unfortunately, health care providers often neglect this critical issue. The stigma continues.

In my workshops, I share the story of how, in an instant, I changed from a pretty lady into a lady who looked like a mummy lying in a hospital bed, unconscious, in a coma for nearly two months. I show them how the evolution of this experience transformed me into the person I am today and how physical difference has no bearing on the value of a person.

As the first burn survivor appointed to the North Carolina Jaycee Burn Center advisory board, I contributed to developing and funding an exemplary aftercare program for burn survivors. Aftercare, as defined by the Burn Center, encompasses meeting the patients' and their families' emotional and psychosocial needs and educating them about what to expect along the extensive road of recovery. Importantly, it offers opportunities and tools necessary to heal and to make the most positive transition from burn victim to burn survivor.

Annually, the Burn Center hosts a "Celebration of Life," bringing together survivors, loved ones, burn care professionals, and fire service members for a day of fellowship and inspiration. In 2003, that's where I met Marsha Lowe, one of six children who survived a catastrophic fire and burns at Flat Rock School in Mt. Airy, North Carolina, in 1957. Clothing covered nearly every inch of Marsha's body, making it impossible to determine the extent of her burns. But her exuberant smile hid a deeper secret—unresolved issues associated with her changed body. She'd been hiding her scars this way for more than forty years.

In *Tragedy to Triumph*, a book by Randle E. Brim about Marsha and the other five fire survivors, Randle describes Marsha's encounter with me in this way:

> Charlene Pell's presence struck Marsha's attention immediately. Charlene was wearing a sleeveless blouse.
>
> Marsha said, "Her fingernails, like mine, were burned, rough, and cracked, yet they were painted. Her eyebrows were softly drawn on and looked so natural. She was such a quiet, soft-spoken lady! She was humble, self-assured, and completely comfortable with accepting herself as she was. It was obvious that she was happy with herself."
>
> Marsha said, "How brave she is!"
>
> Marsha thought, *If she can be that comfortable with herself, then I could be!*
>
> Marsha came away from that meeting, and meeting Charlene, with her head held high and an inner peace that she didn't know she was missing. The radiation of Charlene Pell as a complete person still stands out in Marsha's mind. Marsha said, "I will always thank Charlene for her gift of self-confidence she gave me."

Marsha's kind and thoughtful remarks touched me deeply. I was overcome with joy to know that I could help Marsha conquer her fear of showing her scars so that she could be free to confidently wear whatever she chooses.

About a year into my recovery, burn survivors Alan Breslau (founder of the Phoenix Society) and James Partridge (founder of Changing Faces) showed me that it is possible to be confident, successful, and attractive even with disfiguring scars. Because of what I learned from them, I have been able to pass along this magnificent gift to many burn survivors and others throughout the years. When you change your attitude and accept your scars and disfigurement and understand that they are now "a part of" who you are, but not "who you are"—and you refuse to allow society to determine who you are—scars will not prevent you from wearing what you want to wear, or from doing whatever you want to do.

In my work, I have encountered thousands of people living with disfigurement. I have heard many stories of personal and professional rejection and discrimination because of facial differences. Often, well-qualified candidates apply for jobs online and move through the process well, until prospective employees appear for in-person interviews. However, once the potential employer discovers the applicant's facial difference, the applicant falls out of favor, even when they are equally or more qualified for the position. One of my dearest friends experienced this while seeking employment after his burn injury.

Employers are reluctant to hire people with disfigurement because they do not want to put other employees, clients, or customers in situations where they might feel uneasy. Authentic media representations could help change public perceptions and attitudes about those living with a facial difference.

Beyond emergency medical care, people with facial differences deserve access to peer support and therapy as needed to help them reenter society in whatever way they can. Children and adults with visible differences are often stigmatized and face much psychosocial adversity. Social attitudes, bias, and beliefs have a direct impact on the development of these individuals. The physical depictions of "good" and "attractive" people in various media, including literature, films, advertisements, paintings, and photographs, shape and influence social norms. Children with visible differences are rarely portrayed positively in children's literature or media. There's a severe shortage of quality books that authentically characterize children with visible differences.

As a member of Face Equality International (FEI), a social justice movement devoted to ensuring that those with facial differences live freely, without indignity or discrimination, I advocate for this neglected human rights issue that affects nearly one hundred million people worldwide.

In an ideal world, nondisabled/nondisfigured people would accept and appreciate people with disfiguring conditions. However, this most likely will be difficult to achieve. The stigma ingrained in society is so pervasive and so perpetuated by the media that it will be challenging, but not impossible, to change attitudes and perceptions about those with visible differences. Still, my work to change attitudes through education, advocating for authentic media representation, and helping others with disfiguring conditions individually or in my workshops gives purpose to my life. My work makes a difference, even if I change one heart at a time.

Like many others, I continue to experience pain, discomfort, physical challenges, and burn-related procedures. Yet this ongoing, heart-wrenching ordeal has taught me that I have the strength and fortitude to press forward through my disappointment and suffering to find purpose and joy in my life. All my experiences, before and after the accident, have shaped me into the woman I am today.

Despite what we think we can or can't do, all of us can endure circumstances that appear daunting or impossible or things that we pray will never happen to us. We have the innate capacity to adapt and to get through unthinkable challenges to live meaningful, full lives—and, if it is our wish to do so, to achieve extraordinary things.

Author's Note

Since my unfortunate experience at the ABA in 1996, a significant milestone occurred in 2007, when the ABA created the Aftercare Reintegration Committee (ARC), which combines the expertise of ABA and Phoenix Society professionals to coordinate their efforts to establish standards of aftercare rehabilitation and reintegration for those affected by burn trauma (Corry et al., 2009). The ARC aims to identify the best ways for the ABA and the Phoenix Society to collaborate on creating clinical care programs and research priorities. Today, the ABA and the Phoenix Society collaborate on projects aligning with their missions.

Moreover, the National Institute on Disability, Independent Living, and Rehabilitation Research (NIDILLR, formerly NIDRR) has been a primary funder of burn rehabilitation research to improve the lives of burn survivors. It stipulates research on the long-term effects of burn injury and identification of the needs of burn survivors in functional outcomes, health and rehabilitation services, and community reintegration (Goverman, et al., 2017; Corry et al., 2009).

Patients and their families are considered essential collaborators in the process, and the ABA and the ARC personify this patient-provider collaboration (Corry et al., 2009).

Burn survivors are welcome at annual ABA conferences; they present and publish research and serve on ABA committees, and a few have been recognized with prestigious awards for their contributions to burn prevention and care.

Acknowledgments

Thirty years ago, God spared my life; there is no rational explanation for how Roger and I made our way out of the dense brush forty feet from the runway after I had sustained second- and third-degree burns on 64 percent of my body. Moreover, my burn surgeons attributed my survival and recovery to a force greater than medicine. Some said my sister's unrelenting conviction that I would live willed me back to life! God also blessed me with the most devoted, loving, and caring mother, "DP," and sister, Melissa, to see me through this horrible, painful, prolonged ordeal. Their steadfast love and encouragement sustained me through years of rehabilitation and many setbacks. They made enormous personal and financial sacrifices to stay by my side for nearly two years. Mom died in 2020 after a prolonged and heart-wrenching battle with cognitive vascular dementia. I am eternally grateful to her for allowing me to experience failure and disappointment, to learn how to rebound and carry on after heartbreak and upset. Loving aunts, uncles, and cousins, especially Aunt Ruth and Linda Reavis, were always ready to help in any way.

Of paramount importance is the love, support, and encouragement of my husband, CH, who believes in me and goes out of his way to help no matter what project, goal, or dream I'm pursuing! It would have been impossible to write this book without him. I lovingly call him "Mr. Fix It" because he can repair and restore almost anything, including me!

It has taken me twenty years to complete this memoir,

and many people have encouraged and helped me in numerous ways. Initially, I developed the book as a self-help resource. Friends Ken Irwin and Donna Wilson graciously read and shared my manuscript with an associate working in the publishing business who offered critical feedback, suggested other reading, and said I should consider writing a memoir instead, as readers would only be eager to buy a self-help book from someone with credentials. Meanwhile, my favorite ENT, Dr. Miltich, said, "You're wearing your credentials!" Nevertheless, I rewrote the book as a memoir.

Along the way, I had the good fortune of meeting author Sam Horn through the Florida Speakers Association. Sam told me about the National Speakers Association and the Maui Writers Conference, an extraordinary gathering of agents, editors, publishers, screenwriting professionals, and writers. I participated in a writing workshop with bestselling author and professor Katherine Ramsland. She taught me a crucial lesson: "The art of writing is rewriting," and it's hard work. I also had the privilege of consulting with Susan Crawford and am grateful for her support. Early in 2012, I met Sarah Atkinson at a Proverbs 21 Conference; she graciously gave me some thoughtful, constructive suggestions for my book proposal and encouragement.

Years later, I met author and writing consultant Louise Nayer at a regional burn conference. The daughter of parents horrifically burned in an accident while vacationing when she was a child, she had written a compelling memoir, *Burned.* It was about growing up with disfigured parents and the psychological and emotional impact their burns and experiences had on her life. We immediately connected, and I began to consult with Louise, who taught me how to create vivid, multifaceted scenes. Later, Kathryn Craft, a highly skilled developmental editor and author, helped me excavate feelings and experiences buried in my past and psyche, always focusing on moving the story forward. My friend, editor, and journalist Denise Sicking generously edited the book's first version. While at graduate school at UNC-Greensboro, Dr. Poulos taught me to write more evocatively.

I thank Jane Friedman for replying to my numerous emails about publishing after my traditional book deal collapsed for unknown reasons. Your experience and unparalleled knowledge of all aspects of publishing have helped me beyond measure.

If not for Nathaniel Gilbert's quick response at the scene of the accident, Roger and I would have perished. I would not be alive today without the lifesaving actions of pilots Robby Brady and André Dussault and physicians Jack Kihm and the late Bill Skellenger; without hesitation, they jumped in to help.

The skilled, specially trained trauma burn surgeons, nurses, and specialists at the Ryder Trauma Center/Jackson Memorial Hospital, Miami, Florida, continued the lifesaving procedures and treatments that kept me alive. I thank everyone there for the expert, compassionate care, support, and encouragement, even years after my discharge. Some of these caregivers became friends and colleagues. I sincerely thank Dr. Gillon Ward, founder and medical director of the Burn Center, Dr. Michael Peck, associate director, and Drs. Fernandez and Namias. They cared for me for months through numerous near-death experiences and fourteen surgeries. Dr. David Tse, an internationally recognized surgeon at Bascom Palmer Eye Institute, performed delicate eyelid surgery to protect my cornea from permanent damage. Dr. Rogachefsky performed numerous operations to improve the range of motion and function of my arms and hands. Expert dermatologist Dr. Anne Burdick treated me for several years for issues related to my scalp. I am indebted to Drs. Telischi, my ENT; Stewart Bitman, my gastroenterologist; Harold Landa, my pulmonologist; and many other specialists unknown to me, including phlebotomists, radiologists, respiratory specialists, anesthesiologists, and nutritionists, who played a vital role in my care while I was comatose.

Occupational therapist Angel Alvarez eased my fears and made me laugh through countless unpleasant procedures. Physical therapist Sharon Eisenberg pushed me to do more daily. At the same time, nurses Elizabeth, Maria, Cindy, Melissa Hall, and many others attended to dressing changes, pain management, and personal needs. Maria somehow picked up on the fact that I had been studying Spanish for several years and spoke to me in Spanish. Even though I didn't understand most of what she said, I appreciated the gesture; I felt her care and concern for me. A burly fellow on the night shift heard about my love of jazz, so he played music for me. I thank social worker Rolando for telling Melissa about the Phoenix Society for Burn Survivors and for assisting Mom and Melissa while I was at Jackson Memorial, and Olga Quintana for her support throughout the years.

Dr. Eddie Sassoon, physiatrist at HealthSouth Sunrise Rehabilitation Hospital (HSSRH), was one of the most compassionate, caring physicians I had ever encountered. He listened to my concerns and worked to provide every treatment and accommodation I requested. He welcomed my participation in planning my rehabilitation and respected my input. I'll also never forget and always be grateful for psychologist Dr. "Mic" Rathjens. Thank you for helping me come to terms with my altered body and devastating personal and professional losses, for listening to and acknowledging my frustrations, and for showing me that I could live a happy, purposeful life and maybe experience love again after my injury and disfigurement. Thank you for recording my favorite music and giving me the tapes to soothe my pain and suffering. I'll never forget your thoughtfulness and genuine concern.

Howard Neuman, you big teddy bear of a man, thank you for bringing touch back to my life, for easing my discomfort and pain through targeted, gentle massage, and for listening to my concerns.

Nurse Marilyn Frail, you cared for me as if I might be your sister. Thank you for your compassionate, skilled care and for sharing your delicious home-cooked meals. I am grateful to all the nurses caring for me at HSSRH. I will never forget Joyce Farghusen, the Jamaican angel who stayed with and comforted me throughout the first frightening weeks at HSSRH. I treasure the poignant poem written for me by nurse Julia Howell. She captured the magnitude of my suffering and losses in her poetry. Nurses Robin Tenenbaum, Althea Foster, and so many others whose names I can't recall, thank you for your compassionate, competent care.

Occupational therapist Adrienne Lauer, thank you for always making me laugh or smile during our sessions. With gratitude, I remember my hand-therapy sessions with Sandi Cox and Linda Alfieri; thank you for sharing stories with me during my treatment sessions to take my mind off the pain and for your ongoing friendship. Thanks to physical therapists Pete and Margaret for helping me regain my strength, stamina, and mobility.

I was blessed to have had many extraordinary caregivers. I would not be where I am today without them, and I am eternally grateful to each one of them. I know I have unintentionally omitted compassionate, skilled nurses, therapists, aides, specialists, and technicians who treated me at Jackson Memorial and HSSRH, particularly those who cared for me while I was comatose. Please forgive me and know that if you contributed to my recovery and rehabilitation in any way, I am eternally grateful.

After discharge from HSSRH, Tami Seltman, OTR/L, CHT, at the Fort Lauderdale Hand Clinic, helped me regain essential use of my fused and contracted fingers. During that time, I also discovered psychologist Dr. Patricia Georgoff. I knew we would connect when I saw her sticky notepad reading "Toto, I've a feeling we're not in Kansas anymore!" Thirty years later, I keep something she wrote on one of these notepads under the glass on my desk. It reads that what happens to you emotionally will be expressed physiologically unless there is a therapeutic intervention. She taught me this invaluable lesson. She also introduced me to visualization and stress-reducing techniques I still use today.

Michael E. Kelly is an exceptional plastic surgeon who worked diligently to restore my facial features. He is also one of only two surgeons among many to personally call me hours after a surgical procedure to check on me. I'm also thankful for Dr. Molnar's expertise, thoughtfulness, and support.

I am blessed to have an extraordinary, caring, delightful ophthalmologist, Dr. Giegengack, who cares for my vision. I am most grateful for my oculoplastic surgeon, Dr. Molly Fuller, who enabled me to close my right eyelid and protect my cornea.

There are those rare, kind, gentle, dependable home-health nurses who brighten your every day, and Rita Miller was mine. She was so sweet and endearing.

During years of rehabilitation, I was fortunate to receive treatment from several outstanding massage therapists, Charlotte Beal, Tammy Bartlett, Heather McLachlan, and Cindy Livingston. Personal trainer Frances Horna always pressed me to do more to improve my strength and endurance.

Years later, my interest in integrative medicine that addresses the mental, physical, and spiritual aspects of health led me to Belleruth Naparstek. To this day, her guided imagery soothes my pain, anxiety, and stress more effectively than anything. We became friends and colleagues.

I'll always cherish the night I met Nancy Ogden West, a professional makeup artist. I had been invited to be her model for the evening, to demonstrate camouflage cosmetics. She was kind and considerate and skillfully applied foundation, powder, eye shadows, and blush as she described each technique to a group of cosmetologists. Once she finished, she handed me a mirror. I was overcome with emotion to see my transformation. The bright-red splotches of skin on my face blended with the predominant flesh color, and the red raised scars were less noticeable. I felt relieved knowing I could blend in with others and not generate unwanted attention from curious strangers.

I am indebted to my former boss and executive vice president of DCOTA, Joan Kerns, and the founder, the late Marvin Danto, and to Jim Danto; I lovingly referred to Marvin as "Mr. D." Every time he saw my mom at the hospital, he placed a one-hundred-dollar bill in the palm of her hand. I am so grateful to my colleagues at DCOTA, especially Chris Sarko Kerns, Carol Fullwood, Javier Rivera, Gus DelPoso, Vikki Reinitz, and Mike Armbruster, for donating blood for my ongoing transfusions. Thank you to my friend and confidante Carol Naveira-Nicholson, an exceptional flutist and invaluable word processing administrator wiz! Thank you to Janet Roda, Kate Lacusky, Jan Carberry, Darcel Avello, Lisa Puccio, and Blanca Romero for your cards, gifts, meals, encouragement, and visits to support and cheer me on while I was hospitalized.

Thank you, Jim and Chris Kerns, for nudging me out of my comfort zone to do a reading at your wedding. It launched me into a professional speaking and workshop career.

Gracias a Rita Frohlich, mi profesora fabulosa de español.

I'm grateful to the retired attorney Barry Meadow of Podhurst Orseck and to his assistant, Mirtha. I'm eternally thankful to David Katzman for being an extraordinary aviation attorney, for believing in and representing me, and for vetting the text about the airplane and legal references. Donna Mooney and Lisa Forsell, thank you for assisting me with Mr. Katzman, and Don Sommer, thank you for being an unparalleled aviation investigator. I am grateful to Carolyn Schurr-Levine for vetting portions of the memoir.

A heartfelt thank you to the colleagues who helped to propel my speaking career and workshops: Bonnie Wesorick, Jacinta Burchett, Cathy Mackie, and Barbara Hodge. Blake Engel, thank you for including me in your documentary *Rising Phoenix*. I am grateful to Dalton Cox for generously volunteering time and expertise to edit hours of film for my documentary, *Down in Flames, Up in Love*. Thank you to Dave Sluyter for inviting me to participate in the Fetzer Institute's Relationship-Centered Care initiative and for featuring my story in *The Stories: Experiences of Relationship-Centered Care*, an educational resource created for health care professionals. I cherish the times spent at the Fetzer Institute. I sincerely appreciate Kathleen Bogart, PhD, for her generosity and support of my work. Dr. Jessica McCall has also been an enthusiastic ally. And a heartfelt thank you to Canice Crerand, PhD, who is a colleague I can always count on. Ann Starrette, thank you for your friendship and for creating a beautiful, sacred space for contemplation and spiritual growth.

My dear associates and friends pastor Shirley Massey; Anita Mareday Fields, RN; and Mary Kessler, RN; are exceptional UNC health care providers who have championed aftercare for burn survivors and their loved ones for decades. Thank you, Mary Coffey, RN, PhD, nursing manager and specialist at Virginia Commonwealth University, for your support and commitment to aftercare for burn survivors.

Dana Jordan, publisher of *Lake Norman Woman* magazine, thank you for selecting me as the inaugural winner of the magazine's Women of Will contest—a recognition and surprise I'll always treasure—and for your ongoing support of my work. A very special thank you to Deb Kaclik, former director of social and emotional learning and behavior support for Charlotte-Mecklenburg Schools, and John King, former counselor at Greensboro Day School, for recognizing the value of "Outside, Inside; You Decide," my workshop for middle school students to foster acceptance and appreciation of differences, and for the opportunity to present the workshop in Charlotte-Mecklenburg and Guilford County Schools. Deborah Young, thank you for volunteering your time and talent and photography to causes important to me.

I couldn't have done my work for the Phoenix Society without my fun-loving, efficient, and creative administrative assistant, Marie Kenyon. Her wit and willingness were invaluable. Later, a sweet, dear young woman, Annie India, helped me juggle everything. She and her mother, Prudence, became friends. I am grateful for the dearest friends and mentors I found and cherish through the Phoenix Society: Delwyn Breslau, George and Jo Anne Pessotti, Rick and Mary Halpert, Janet Harman, and Dennis Gardin, the host of the first World Burn Congress I attended, and so many others. We remain in close contact twenty-eight years later! I'm indebted to the late Alan Breslau, James Partridge, and Frank McGonagle, my earliest burn survivor mentors. For every burn survivor or person with a disfigurement with whom I've met or worked, you have touched me and my life, and I hope I have made a positive difference in your lives. We are exceptional, strong, and resilient people who have endured and overcome unimaginable physical and emotional pain.

I'm indebted to pastors Dr. Dwayne Black and the late Jack Noble; Bob Miller, Mom's pastor at the time of the accident; and the members of Center United Methodist Church, whose love, prayers, cards, and gifts uplifted and blessed us for months. I'm grateful for the First United Methodist Church of Miami, which welcomed Mom and Melissa during those uncertain, scary weeks when I teetered on death.

Thank you to my friends Mark and Annie Nadler, Jean Luc, and Renatta Ferrigno for being there for me, especially during the first year after the crash and losing Roger. I am grateful to Billie and Connie Hughes, Roger's dearest lifelong friends, who stood by me throughout my recovery. I'm thankful I met Valerie Delroy at a Tony Robbins conference that gave me a boost when I most needed it. Torsten and Marianne Rundgren, I'm so glad you couldn't be on that fateful flight with us; I sincerely appreciate your kindness and friendship. Maria Elizabeth Lechuge, I always looked forward to seeing you when you came to help me with household chores, and I loved your sister, Blanca Romero.

Dearest lifelong friends Rachel and Ernie sent encouraging cards weekly. They and their daughter, Emma-Li, are family and have always been close by whenever we needed them.

I'm blessed to have the loyal support of lifelong friends Christine Calice, Peggy Reilly Smith, and Debbie Hinson. We've shared so many fun and poignant experiences since middle school. My wise, insightful friend Mary Jo Greil has been a source of enlightenment and encouraged me to write this book for years. Author, professor, and my sister-in-law, Paula Connolly, PhD, has cheered me on and assisted in all my endeavors.

Linda Perry, my dear friend and former associate, I'm thrilled to have found you and reconnected after all these years!

To my beloved best friend, Debra Buzzell, thank you for your sage advice, for always being there for me, and for your wit and wisdom. You are always a voice of reason to me. Thank you and your friend Gloria MacKenzie for reading and critiquing my book and not holding back. Your questions and comments improved the book.

Pam Atkins, thank you for always being available momentarily to step in and help me care for Mom during her last years. I don't know what I would have done without you!

And Doreen Coulter, thank you for being the kindest, most thoughtful neighbor who catered to our every need for three weeks while we suffered through COVID-19.

I'm thankful to Randy Barnes for creating and managing my websites and donating much of his work. I'm grateful to Joey Seawell for my fabulous untouched photos and for being a dear neighbor to Mom.

I treasure my first burn survivor friend, Kevin McGann, and his witty wife, Nancy, and their extraordinary daughter, Serena. We have been friends for thirty years!

I'm so grateful for my first hairdresser after the injury, Lucie. She worked wonders with my sprigs of hair as it grew back with a different texture. Deborah Johnson, my delightful nail technician, became a trusted friend.

And a special thank you to my dear nieces, Carlene (Carly) Krupa, Machenta Ramdeholl, and Katherine George, who say I'm the "best aunt ever."

I am grateful to Girl Friday Productions for partnering with me to publish my book. I had a superb team of professionals committed to quality bookmaking, including Christina Henry de Tessan, vice president of strategic partnerships; Kristin Duran, publishing manager; Georgie Hockett, marketing director; Paul Barrett, art director; Emily Weigel, cover designer; Jaye Whitney Debber, senior production editor; Abi Pollokoff, editorial manager; Janice Lee, production editor; and the exacting copyeditor, Carrie Urbanic; and Melody Moss, proofreader.

For twenty years, I loved and envisioned the title of my book as *Down in Flames, Up in Love*, as suggested by author Sam Horn. Kristin recommended the title *In This Altered Body*, with a subtitle. It's perfect! Throughout the book, I use this phrase to describe my body after the burn injury.

To everyone who reads this book: I hope there will be something that resonates with you, uplifts you, helps you

endure adversity, unexpected setbacks, or sorrows, and re-
minds you that more than you can imagine is possible with
hope, faith, and love; anything is possible!

Resources

If you or a loved one has a facial difference or disfiguring condition, the following organizations may be of help:

- AboutFace: https://aboutface.ca, @aboutface
- American Cleft Palate Craniofacial Association: https://acpacares.org, @ACPAcares
- Burn Survivors of New England: https://www.bsone.org
- Changing Faces: https://www.changingfaces.org.uk, @FaceEquality
- Children's Craniofacial Association (CCA Kids, USA): https://ccakids.org, @CCAKidsTweet
- ConnectMed International, USA: https://connectmed.org, @connectmed
- Courageous Faces Foundation: https://courageousfacesfoundation.org, @courageousfaces
- Face Equality International: https://faceequalityinternational.org, @FaceEqualityInt
- FACES: National Craniofacial Association: https://www.faces-cranio.org, @faces_cranio
- Facing Forward: https://facingforwardinc.org, @FacingForwardUS
- Life After Burns: https://www.lifeafterburns.ca, @LifeAfterBurns
- Mamingwey Burn Survivor Society, Canada: https://mamingwey.ca, @Mamingwey

- Many Faces of Moebius Syndrome, USA:
  https://manyfacesofmoebiussyndrome.org,
  @team_moebious
- Moebius Syndrome Foundation, USA: https://
  moebiussyndrome.org, @MoebiusSyndrome
- MyFace, USA: https://www.myface.org,
  @thisis_myface
- Phoenix Society for Burn Survivors: https://www
  .phoenix-society.org, @PSburnsurvivors
- Smile Foundation: https://smilefoundationsa.org,
  @smilefoundation
- Smile Train: https://www.smiletrain.org,
  @Smiletrain
- Transforming Faces, Canada: https://transform
  ingfaces.org, @TransformFaces

References

ADA National Network (2015) "Disability Awareness and Nondiscrimination." In: *A Planning Guide for Making Temporary Events Accessible to People with Disabilities,* edited by Cynthia Saltzman and Rebecca Matter. https://adata.org/guide/planning-guide-making-temporary-events-accessible-people-disabilities.

Anti-Defamation League (2016) "Talking to Young Children about Bias and Prejudice." https://www.adl.org/education/resources/tools-and-strategies/talking-to-young-children-about-bias-and-prejudice.

Braithwaite, Dawn O., and Teresa L. Thompson (2000) *Handbook of Communication and People with Disabilities: Research and Application.* Mahwah, NJ: Lawrence Erlbaum Associates.

Brim, Randle E. (2007) *Tragedy to Triumph.* Asheboro, NC: Piedmont Printing, p.228.

Centers for Disease Control and Prevention. *Disability Impacts All of Us.* Accessed September 9, 2022. https://www.cdc.gov/ncbddd/disabilityandhealth/infographic-disability-impacts-all.html.

Corry, Nida, Thomas Pruzinsky, and Nichola Rumsey (2009) "Quality of Life and Psychosocial Adjustment to Burn Injury: Social Functioning, Body Image, and Health Policy Perspectives," *International Review of Psychiatry* 21, no. 6, pp. 539–48. https://www.researchgate.net

/publication/38095020_Quality_of_life_and
_psychosocial_adjustment_to_burn_injury_Social
_functioning_body_image_and_health_policy
_perspectives/link/0deec53731e53229ae000000
/download?_tp=eyJjb250ZXh0Ijp7ImZpcnN0UG
FnZSI6InB1YmxpY.

Deegan, Mary Jo (1977) "The Non-verbal Communication of
the Physical Handicapped," *Journal of Sociology & Social
Welfare* 4, no. 5 (article 4). http://scholarworks.wmich
.edu/jssw/vol4/iss5/4.

Face Equality International. "About FEI." Accessed September
8, 2022. https://faceequalityinternational.org.

Goverman, Jeremy, Katie Mathews, Radha K. Holavanahalli,
Andrew Vardanian, David N. Herndon, Walter J.
Meyer, Karen Kowalske, Jim Fauerbach, Nicole S.
Gibran, Gretchen J. Carrougher, Dagmar Amtmann,
Jeffrey C. Schneider, and Colleen M. Ryan (2017) "The
National Institute on Disability, Independent Living, and
Rehabilitation Research Burn Model System: Twenty
Years of Contributions to Clinical Service and Research."
Journal of Burn Care & Research 38(1): e240-e253. e253,
https://doi.org/10.1097/BCR.0000000000000361.

Hyde, Michael J. (2006) *The Life-Giving Gift of
Acknowledgement: A Philosophical and Rhetorical
Inquiry.* West Lafayette, IN: Purdue University Press, p. 1.

Koncius, Jura (June 13, 2017) "It's a Southern Thing: Why
So Many Porch Ceilings Are Blue." *Washington Post*,
Home & Garden. https://www.washingtonpost.com
/lifestyle/home/its-a-southern-thing-why-so-many
-porch-ceilings-are-blue/2017/06/12/f6299014-3b3a
-11e7-9e48-c4f199710b69_story.html.

Phillips, Don (July 18, 1999) "Conditions Difficult for Kennedy Flight." *Washington Post*, A19. https://www .washingtonpost.com/wp-srv/national/longterm/jfkjr /stories/crash071899.htm.

Rhode, Deborah L. (May 23, 2010) "Why Looks Are the Last Bastion of Discrimination." *Washington Post*, B4. https://www.washingtonpost.com/wp-dyn/content/ article/2010/05/20/AR2010052002298.html.

Wikipedia. "John Dewey: Education and Teacher Education." Accessed September 9, 2022. https://en.wikipedia.org /wiki/John_Dewey.

About the Author

Charlene Pell is the founder and executive director of Facing Forward, a nonprofit organization dedicated to helping individuals with congenital or acquired facial or physical differences contend with staring, improve control of social interactions, and communicate confidently. Thirty years ago, Pell survived a catastrophic plane crash that burned 64 percent of her body, severely injuring her face and hands.

As a result of her disfigurement and the lack of psychosocial resources available to her during her recovery, Pell researched and created programs and resources to help herself and others adjust to their changed appearance and circumstances. Since 1998, she's shared her insights as a keynote speaker at conferences for burn survivors and healthcare professionals. She created a nationwide program titled "What to Do When People Stare: A Workshop to Teach Individuals with Disfiguring Conditions to Contend With Staring and Improve Control of Social Interactions." Her work has been published in *Skin, Psychology Today,* the American Burn Association's *Journal of Burn Care & Research,* and other periodicals.

Before her accident, Pell was vice president of communications for one of the most prominent design centers in the United States, the Design Center of the Americas. She managed and administered its marketing strategy and created extensive public relations programs in cooperation with *Architectural Digest, House Beautiful, Interior Design,* and many other publications. Pell has a master's in communication studies from the University of North Carolina at Greensboro. She lives in Greensboro, North Carolina, with her husband.

Milton Keynes UK
Ingram Content Group UK Ltd.
UKHW011121050624
443649UK00006B/453